The Eng. Lit. Kit.

Diggory Tweedcroft was born into literature right from the moment of his delivery on a hastily cleared table in Stratford Municipal library. Up at Cambridge by the age of six, he was moved over to Oxford after shooting a corporation swan in a private and controversial attempt to understand 'The Ancient Mariner'. His PhD at Oxford, 'The Effect of the Menopause on George Eliot's Later Novels' was eventually translated into one language and has become a virtual starting point in the field of The Older Novelist. He swiftly followed this with the highly acclaimed 'Absolutely Percolated: Coffee and The Eighteenth Century Couplet', a success which gained him the Detritus Professorship at Wash-on-the-Waffle. People who'd never thought of seeing literature through the workings of the human body flocked from California and Sweden to hear him, whilst critics began to talk of 'The Tweedcroft Revolution'. Meanwhile Professor Tweedcroft worked on in the seclusion of cycling round his caravan on the college carpark, reading aloud with a yard of port. It was during the circumnavigation of his most recent work that he met the biradial passion of his life, Boadicea, a drop-handlebar tourer whose support carried him onto new highways with 'The School of British Leyland: Studies in Austen and Morris'. For his next work his caravan was cordoned off. His hobbies are being brilliant, absent-minded, colour-blind and utterly untidy, and he still retains a life-long fear of the motor car. Diggory Tweedcroft is not married and has four children.

THE
ENG
LIT
KIT

Professor Diggory Tweedcroft
and Dr Duff Wimpole

ARROW BOOKS

To Dot, Pa & Baby Harwood

Arrow Books Limited
17–21 Conway Street, London W1P 6JD

An imprint of the Hutchinson Publishing Group

London Melbourne Sydney Auckland
Johannesburg and agencies throughout
the world

First published in 1982 by The Garrick Press

Arrow edition 1984

Set in Linotron Plantin
by Input Typesetting Ltd, London
Printed and bound in Great Britain
by The Guernsey Press Co Ltd
Guernsey, C.I.

ISBN 0 09 938190 7

Contents

Preface

I would like to record my indebtedness to the following, who at various stages in the book's composition have been invaluable: the staff of Pidgin College English Library, for the personal opening hours during which I was able to read fortissimo, unhindered by all those little murmurs and rustlings of paper which can be so distracting; the College Bicycle Attendant, Mr. Eric Noak, for many gallant afternoons in the pits when my chosen path with Boadicea was not all that it might have been; my father, for a long-term strategy on punctuation; the late Professor Ambrose Firewick, for helping me over a sticky patch in my grasp of the Romantics, by consuming historic quantities of hashish, laudanum and cocaine; my mother, for intimate sartorial back-up and regular parcels of firm fruit. Any errors that remain are thus not entirely my own fault.

D.T.

Anglosaxonica

We can't be sure when English Literature will end, and we don't really know when it started. But we have found out – whatever Chaucer says – that there were at least six hundred years of it before him. Nearly all of it is anonymous, and this is pretty understandable while a good deal of it, mercifully, has been lost or eaten (oral literature). What remains to us we call Anglo-Saxon literature i.e. about thirty thousand lines on four dragon-scorched manuscripts.

These manuscripts have withstood the test of time longest, and so there are scholars who believe they constitute the best works of art. This is a suspiciously subjective view as the scholars themselves tend to be much older than anyone else. But right up to the day when they fall off a library chair for the last time, they have been winkling out editions of these lines, complete with dictionaries, maps of journeys, reconstructions of battles, artists' impressions of the monsters involved, supplies of eye-wash and caffeine pills. Twelve volumes alone conduct a riveting discussion of the word 'tarf' in 1.65 of MS IV, concluding that the word is more likely to belong to a shaggy-dog story than a monologue, and is probably an anagram of the Old English 'fart'.

Frankly, never has so much been written by so ancient about so few. Coltish young students have voiced the opinion that if the Anglo-Saxons got the literature they deserved, what did *they* ever do to deserve having to study it? Well, let's not have a row on the second page – and besides the Normans will come and put a stop to it before long. In fact, on page 17.

The Ancient Britons had agriculture, horticulture but no real culture. The best they could do was to paint each other and write on women: 'if hic manthyng reomin, heddclub till homein.'

So the Angles, Saxon and Newts landed with stocks of quills, inkhorns and parchment as soon as they could.

The Newts were always terrifically drunk. No-one knows where they came from, least of all themselves, being much too fond of mead to be vertical or coherent for long enough to speak, let alone write. If ever they did write anything down they couldn't remember what or where they'd put it. But amazingly it was the Newts who brought with them our first epic poem about 'Beer Wulf' – a massive and inebriate hound reared beyond their control onto a devastating rampage, and how they finally cornered him and accidentally killed him. The manuscript is intact, but both illegible where the quill has erroneously gone into a beer-horn, and short of several key phrases where the Newt has inadvertently finished his sentence elsewhere. A Newt table discovered

earlier this century at Noggin bears many scratchings, amidst goblet marks and enormous star-shaped stains, which have enabled scholars to complete most of the lines.

In England no literature is attributed to the Newts, but we see them in odd Anglo-Saxon allusions to people being 'Newtered', 'mute as Newts' etc. They also popularised that convenient little conjunction 'hic'. Yet gradually the survival of the soberest relegated tribes of Newts to the far-flung corners of our isles where they have retained their own language and whose descendants have contributed sporadically to our literature ever after. We shall meet some of them later on.

Literature in England, then, was bump-started by the Anglo-Saxons. They were a sad, tough lot – but even they got bored with the same old round of eating, drinking and wenching contests which erupted in the Hall after every victory over their neighbours and miscellaneous dragons.

They wanted a change, something more substantial. So they invented 'potes' and called what they wrote 'potery', to be sung out after dinner. These 'potes' or 'poets', chosen for their proven inadequacy with a sword could be seen standing on nearby hill-tops during battles, making up lines, often chanting aloud. After some early casualties, poets soon realised how to stay alive:

1. Name all the important people who'd turned out e.g. the sons of Offal, Godwig nephew of Godhair etc. AND any particularly large unimportant people who'd asked for a mention e.g. Bertstan.

2. Lose count of the number of people the chief killed. If he likes figures, do not under-estimate by more than ten victims. Up to ten is 'poetic licence' beyond ten is 'poetic absence'.

3. There are no defeats for your tribe. On a bad day, you 'wily wold away'. This sounds like strategy. On absolutely any day when your tribe weren't actually going backwards, the enemy has been 'all blodding outswinged'.

4. Keep an eye out for any stray arrows.

5. With dragons, under-reckoning their size by more than ten feet is dangerous. They, of course, should be terrifying and fit. After all, no dragon-slayer – especially if he's the chief and had a few drinks – really wants to hear what a pathetic show the dragon put up, how despite severe cramp it nearly took his head off countless times before dying of a heart attack.

However, most poems are about exile, for poets were continually being shown the Hall door and told to wander off. It seems these early 'bards' or 'roods' just weren't any good at poetry. But how bad were they? Their rejection by primitive audiences is of course to have no bearing on our judgement. We shall rather examine the texts. So let us rise above the argument of the flying spear advanced by the poets' contemporaries, and scrutinise a few lines composed in exile by a typical 'bard' or 'rood':

> wund ic woruld   weariz min lod
> for ic wunderwroth   ond frigging freosan
> no mete ni medodrinc   months onend
> wold ic hin   neck wring wurm
> hearpe hefi   ond hungrig ond wifless
> signsic bin ic   of NO ROODS NO WICINGS
> ond wot wyrs iz   whopping dreagon
> her along corms cwist cwic..........

Although badly scorched, the manuscript is a typical 'Fitt': lines never begin with a capital letter, punctuation is ignored, words are mis-spelt and none of them rhyme.* The student might object that modern poetry is the same, but really you can't expect to get away with that sort of thing at the start of Literature. It's all right when you're good, or nowadays, but roods were both ancient and awful and definitely pushing their luck.

Closing our eyes to the movingly vulgar choice of word, let us dip generally into Anglo-Saxon word construction for a moment. Basically, they amalgamated lots of little words where we would use one: feast, becomes 'stufface', sword 'headoffthyng', consummation 'withalling', death 'bucketkikt', winter 'brassdreagonweather' and so on. You could even make up your own, if careful to remember that the Anglo-Saxons enacted their words with appropriate gestures. For example, a short stab of the right foot would accompany the word 'bucketkikt' or a roaring face with arms flapping which suddenly changed to hollowed cheeks going 'ooh' as the arms drop and clasp further down, would signify winter.

* Cf. My father's brilliant punctuation of an Anglo-Saxon Fitt in 'What the Hell's All This Then?' by Colon Tweedcroft.

11

Returning to the poem, we have noticed that it doesn't rhyme. However, closer inspection would reveal that the rood is trying to distract our attention from this omission by making as many words as possible start with the same letter. This is extremely primitive, and scholars rightly label it 'illiterative verse'. But it did help the rood's live performance to go on and on and on, in what we shall call the metre of Unrhymed Diameters. It is my intimate favourite for reading aloud – recalling to me, as it does, the music made by a treasured old car of mine – its movement being roughly: Bang / Pop / Seizure / Bang / Crash. This pause or 'seizure' provided the rood with valuable time in which to think how to finish the line. With a rood in top form the seizure would be barely perceptible, but such *bon ton* a rood would have been highly irregular. Normally, he would pause to sip his mead, call for a horn that wasn't cracked, play a lead break on his harp, or drop his harp. If not overdone, he could when really stuck, go out to the toilet – and if hopelessly stuck not come back. But never would a rood return with a simile, metaphor, irony, litotes or any of the other devices one feels better for noticing. By making everything 'illiterate' in simple, staccato syntax roods were being extremely indigenous and thoroughly monotonous.

So far we have kept quiet about something serious: Irish monks. Vaguing around in the North of England bringing potatoes, horses and fire-water to the warriors,

12

they also peddled a line in Christianity, which led to monasteries, apostles, fights and sic more poetry. But the Anglo-Saxons didn't mind: they quite enjoyed the hospitality of Northumbrian monasteries and listened very sympathetically to monks who wanted to get married.

And monks provided yet another service: the taking in of stray manuscripts of all conditions, mattering it not whether misused for wrapping, wedging and scouring all sorts of unsuitable objects, whether charred or half-eaten. Many, of course, have remained lost – and a few people who won't like this chapter are still looking for them. Indeed, a day in the life of a manuscript was a lonely, filthy and defenceless existence until the church clairvoyant took it in and gave it New Life. For it should be said that while God's Hand did nothing for the style of His Monks' poetry It was performing miracles on the content of other peoples' poems. Firstly manuscripts were preserved in stout leather covers and locked in – in case any passing rood should see what was happening

13

to his poem. The doctrine of Transubscription was then applied. Abysmally pagan poems were best put out of their misery and 'sent on ahead'; others, with a little Holy Ink, could be saved.

Fortunately for the opening chapters of literary histories, the Anglo-Saxons had a belief that was easily edited, for their world was ruled by Odd, a weird and ruthless Fate whose nasty quirks made all live in fear of Oddswallop. Notice the discrepancies in a sample redemption:

What the Rood wrote

suppergon stod lod   scowlig ond lifid
kos on hondred kin   kikt bocket
spaec hin spittig   ov sonrizplan
thowsond skolls   ta skewer Oddwillin
behyndcom wol we   ond backbash
wily yaz waggonlod   ov monks
neow alle swigswift   ond showt Oddsbodikins. . .

After transubscription

suppergon stod lod   skyscanning
kos on hondred kin   in Heaven Godwillin
ond spaec hin softlig   ov sonrizplan
ta offa oneothar   hondred offspringen
wys yaz waggonlod   ov monks
neow alle aftorsayan   Almighticc Advocat . . .

. . .Amen

Some Anglo-Saxons, presumably sated with food, drink, sex AND poetry even got quite interested in religion. However, as far as more poetry is concerned it was now the custom to versify visions of dreams of looking for crosses – at which transcendental geography two monks were far and away the best: Caedmon and Cynewulf. No-one knows who they were, nor exactly what they wrote about, and they might be more than two people but not less than one. Students are advised not to embroider too freely.

At this stage, the student – like most Anglo-Saxons – will be wondering if there's any Prose to read. And there is, if we go to Alfred's Wessex. Alfred, in fact, started

Prose because Poetry wasn't going down too well. But Prose really caught on, and so much so that other chiefs wanted everyone to know they read – hence their names: Ethelred, Guthred, Kenred etc. Those who couldn't read – Wilf the Redeless – went in for oral literature and consumed prodigious amounts to keep up with the others while learning to read. Wanting all his people to read or inwardly digest prose, Alfred the Great (the best reader) started up a newspaper, 'The Anglo-Saxon Chronicle', to which for many years he contributed articles on cookery, sailing, townplanning and himself. Indeed he read so quickly that it wasn't long before he had to start writing. His own books were necessarily books of instruction: 'Boating for Beginners', 'Let's Read', 'Borough Yourself', 'Alfred the Great' etc.

Wessex under Alfred – that rarest of men who can combine warfare and sport with literacy – became something more than Wessex under Alfred. Here was no ordinary warlord, pulverising peasants to bring a small, brooding windswept territory under his cruel dominion. It was as if the very skies of Wessex, characteristically in dark and tangled turmoil were an harbingering metaphor for those stirrings of cultural growth in the late Anglo-Saxon world, stirrings readily comparable with those fructifying scions of civilisation (are you enjoying this sentence?) that flowered with organic (quintessential to all meaningful pronouncements) ease and just a whiff of politics out of Periclean Athens, Medicean Florence and Robin Hood's Nottingham. And all the more amazing when you consider that Alfred was getting really cross with the Danes.

The Danes at home were good sons to their mothers but put them in a group with other lads and let them spend the summer abroad, and they could be REAL BUGGERS. And so it was that these handsome young farmers when they came to England sank into a vortex of crime which is too long to list, but statistically favoured rape, attempted rape, robbery with violence, assault, grievous bodily harm, sailing on the wrong side of the river, failing to stop after burning a village and so

15

on through the whole sad business. They also brought over with them their Norsery Tales which contain such corrupting amounts of violence that it is no wonder they turned out as they did.

So the Danes were a bit of a nuisance, disturbing poetry and prose as well as monopolising 'leaders' in 'The Chronicle' for years on end. What with dragons, hostile neighbours, interfering clerics and Danes, Anglo-Saxon literary culture had a tough time. Prose was doing nicely though, with some of Alfred's best pupils acquiring European reputations as scholars and moralists, and being given a bed in foreign palaces.

Poetry had begun, but such continental trips as roods took were, alas, matters of self-preservation. However, life was still too strange for Fiction and no-one had thought of Drama yet.

Geoffrey Wins Through

The temptation to see 1066 as a convenient dividing line between the Anglo-Saxon and Norman worlds is difficult to resist and therefore won't be resisted. What is also not resisted (because no-one is ever tempted to say it) is that the Norman Conquest was terribly French. They, quite subtly, had heard about English Literature and very discreetly a few of them came over for a read. Their shocked reaction was to invade us at once – whereupon Prose, being far too good, was stopped; and roods, being awful, were arrested. Consequently, anyone who was anyone, or who wanted to be Someone became French – who in their turn, just to be Gallic, decided to become English. This, surprisingly, led to a complete mess where English chaps spoke Franglais and the French spoke Frenglish. Until the compromise of Middle English or Middle French was reached, odd conversations were quite normal. Enter Roger and Pierre, left bank of the Thames:

ROGER: 'How are you going, my dear?'

PIERRE: 'That walks very well, thank you.'

Latin was already over here, courtesy of various monks and scholars, and used mainly to convey theology, science, philosophy, history, medicine and gardening –

while the English language degenerated to a noise made among serfs. The vocabulary of everything else was French-based, particularly when it had something to do with things they were teaching us e.g. law, social climbing, cycling, fashion, love, fencing and polishing. So it is no wonder that historians speak of 'Normania' when you reflect that a scholar who stopped off at the shops on his way to court had to be tri-lingual.

Certain Normaniac phrases have remained with us:

Avoirdupois: Do have some green peas
A la carte: You can have what's on the trolley
Du jambon cru: What was thought to be ham
Faute de mieux: Really my fault
Defense d'Afficher: No Fishing
Hors d'oeuvres: Out of work
Pied-a-terre: One foot in the grave
Chemin de fer: A fur shirt
Attendez moi en bas: Wait for me in stockings
Enjambement: Leg-over
Je ne suis pas de votre avis: I'm not one of your birds
Pas de deux: Father of two

To confuse us totally, the Normans put us in touch with the wisdom of the East, which had spread – following the collapse of Bombay – through North Africa, up the Costa Brava to Monte Carlo where half of it went up the Loire Valley to Paris, and the other half of it got lost. English scholars now had to learn even more languages to catch up with alien theories of Astronomy and a whole variety of new sexual positions.

Prose, however, fell seriously ill: people were just too cowardly or ambitious to confront the Norman ban. But one man would not give in. His name was John Wycliffe or – for he had many aliases and kept on the move – Jean Wyfalaise, Jack Wycliff, Jean-Jacques Pourquoicliff and his work was translating the Bible into English for the first time ever. Furthermore, such an act of defiance brought in the feared Agents of the Pope. Wycliffe went underground. But, wherever he hid the presence of Lollards above ground always gave him away. They were quite unmistakable in their lethargy, leaning on one another or fast asleep in heaps, and the direct cause of various indispositions he received from the Pope's Agents – before finally being excommunicated by a Bull,

at the front of a hit-and-run cart. Yet, till the fatal day, he:

1. Asserted the right of every man to buy a copy of his Bible.
2. Proclaimed the inflammability of the Pope.
3. Refused to believe that seraphims were two rungs higher than cherubims in the order of Angels.
4. Did not understand the meaning of Praeter-transsubstantianionalism.
5. Did not repent calling the Father, Son and The Holy Ghost, The Eternal Triangle.

Was Wycliffe the fearless patriot who wouldn't be gagged? Or the first in a long line of Liturgical Lucrativists who all thought their Bibles would be best-sellers? You could well meet this one 'on the day'.

It was Poetry that Norman *savoir écrire* really fertilised: poets began trying to make their lines fire on the same number of syllables, and rhyme at the end. It was, at first, an experience of wracking intensity. Eager as a young vicar in his first parish, the poet, shooting fingers at the ceiling as he measured out the words, stalked the ends of lines again and again for a rhyme word until, throwing his head almost clean off his shoulders, he would let out the apocalyptic bellow. All poets were happy doing this – well not quite all – as there were still some roods at large who, forced to the North-West of England, had founded RoodRant – a resistance movement to incite an 'Illiterate Revival'. As a venture, its future was already behind it, but against all probability rood poetry died with two enormous bangs: 'Sir Gawain and The Green Knight' and 'Piers' Plowman's.' They depart from the abnorms of rood poetry in a couple of important ways. As one would expect they were anonymous, so people hunted as they frequently did for the roods responsible. What is astonishing is that congratulation seems genuinely to have been the motive for the search. The second shock is that the student will witness a rood handling a major literary device: Allegory. But not an unmitigated shock when you consider that something of the kind had to happen eventually, and that of all the appliances known to Literature, Allegory was destined to be the rood's choice in that the poet doesn't actually mean what he says. You have, in fact, to guess what he meant. But now that Allegory had arrived, it meant two things:

1. 'Rood poetry' was not a term of unqualified abuse.
2. Critical interpreters got to work.

Some affluent and polysyllabic American critics have indeed held that the very word 'Allegory' is substituting for something else, and have filled books guessing what it could stand for. Anyhow, if we discount – as I think we can – that ornamental gap in the Theory of Allegory Studies, let us proceed to take a no-nonsense swipe at what really happens in 'Sir Gawain and The Green Knight', limbering up with a nimble synopsis of the plot.

The Green Knight pops into Camelot at Christmas for a haircut, but as no-one takes any notice of him, he is on the point of leaving when bored, blasé and getting nowhere with Guinevere, suggests if no-one else has the energy, that he could probably manage a trim. When the green client is seated and has outlined the style he'd prefer, Gawain, not paying much attention, decapitates him. Realising what he's done Gawain mumbles an apology. The Green Knight good-humouredly picks up his head, assuring Gawain it's nothing serious and, on the way out, proffers him an invitation to his own establishment next Christmas. When the door is shut, Gawain nonchalantly raises two fingers at it and strolls back to where he left off with Guinevere. Later that night Arthur, on his way to bed, overhears snatches of a hushed conversation in Merlin's room about 'something to loosen her up a bit'.

On the morrow, Arthur insists publicly that the honourable reputation of Camelot obliges Gawain to look for the Green Knight. Good Sir Gawain swearing casually about the likelihood of his moving one inch, suggests that Galahad should go, whereupon a scuffle breaks out.

The same night, when Gawain is swimming thoughtfully in the moat, a horse laden with armour, map, flask and sandwiches wanders out of the gates, which promptly close: the work of a faction led by Arthur. Gawain, sulking, refuses to go anywhere, but moves off a few days later, peevishly doing the exact opposite of whatever the map says. With no audience for his perversity, Gawain soon tires of taking the wrong roads. However, a combination of sightseeing, hangovers and his natural languor, means that he doesn't arrive till Christmas. The Green Knight, in perfect shape apart from the occasional migraine, invites Gawain to a vegetarian meal and dyes his hair green. Gawain returns to Camelot looking bloody silly. The court all think his hair looks great, and the poem ends with everyone scrambling around with buckets and plants, all trying to reproduce that shade of green, while Gawain, picking at an asparagus omelette is hardly able to contain his indifference.

The good student, in a flash, will slot the poem somewhere between a conventional castle-sink drama – say 'Lancelot Come Home' or 'Arthur in Anger' – and a later work of indigenous folk lore, such as 'Jack and the Beanstalk'. For top marks he will allow that elements of both genres apply in the creation of a poem whose veriest, quintessential meaning lies elsewhere – in fact, with ME. (A spectacular drop in marks will await the student who drags someone else into the picture.)

The Green Knight, quite simply, symbolises the power of vegetables to grow again if you lop their heads off at the right time of year: what we may call the Pruning Paradox. Yet it would be premature to dismiss the poem as a melodramatic gardening tip. We now know sufficient about medieval horticulture to realise that pruning was quite within its range, and that it could even show the college gardeners a thing or two – especially how to deal violently with that apparently invincible excrescence which dominates the staff car-park, and from which our feathered friends for too long without challenge have enjoyed an unhygienic advantage over us, our machines and our loved ones. Similarly, I think it would be misguided pedantry to identify the Green Knight as one particular vegetable, though of the candidates which have been presented I would give more credence to 'a tall streak of asparagus' than a 'bunch of watercress', 'an unripe sweetcorn', or a 'big shred of spinach'. If you don't mind how you do in the exams, why not look at an essay by Vergil K. Meredith Jnr. entitled provocatively 'The Green Knight: Animal, Vegetable or Mineral?' (GKS, vol. 58, pp. 315–937) where, after a verdant extravaganza, he wastes no time in putting the case for emeralds and caterpillars. No, the Green Knight is a total and abstract monarch whose amplitude is compromised by identity with any particular, concrete minion. He is the Plant Kingdom and as such (sic), Father Nature as it were.

On the other hand, Gawain and the Court are young human beings, variants on an original model by God, and of quite another substance, colour and texture. Also, it should be remembered that people in those days held positions of responsibility at a much earlier age, so all the lethargy, self-consciousness, sexuality and moodiness of the Court (so beautifully evoked by the poet), is the usual phase for young people not long over the shock of puberty and already into the traumas of adolescence. And, at Camelot, the condition is aggravated by spending too much time indoors. Gawain is chosen by the Green Knight – though he certainly wouldn't put it that way – because he is the only one who leaves the castle for fresh air and exercise (moonlight dips). I incline, therefore, to seeing the Court as symbolic of Meat, whether aggressively killed, sexually violated or endlessly masticated.

We have, then, the two agencies – Plants and Meat– which in 'a bifurcating symbiotic dichotomy' (Hamlet T. Homer Snr.) work for Gawain's spiritual improvement through a series of happenings which we shall elucidate with a Transatlantic model where the angle of the Incident equals the angle of the Abstraction. This all coheres on Gawain's journey: Gawain chases a rabbit (Meat) through the undergrowth (Plants) and into a bog, whence he learns Viscosity and Wisdom; a mouse (Meat) bolts from a hedgerow (Plants) through a gap in Gawain's footwear and round and round inside his armour (Spontaneity); a heavy snowfall covers the landscape (Plants [Latent]), the horse (Meat) refuses to go on, so Gawain builds a snowman (Logic); Gawain seeing a dragon (Meat, lots of it) is blocking the path ahead through the forest (Plants), gives it the chance to escape (Charity); a high wind blows, the plants (Plants) sway, rain pours as Gawain and his horse (Meat) cross the river in flood to go up a mountain (Transience of Youth); a naked prophetess (Meat) rushes out from a bed of nettles (Plants) in front of Gawain, who ignores her (Incompatibility). And so on through the journey to the Green Knight, until Gawain's return as a 'convert' – a disturbingly ironic *choix de mot*. At the end of the poem we see him as a rather priggish vegetarian mystic in a Court still, as yet, on a Meatocentric level of existence. But, from him, the Court will learn how to be natural, for he has seen how Plants, metamorphosed annually or manually, reveal the wise and nutritional resources of Nature. It is a baptism we ignore at our peril in our Meat-laden twentieth century.

The final rood work is (The World According to) 'Piers' Plowman's' and actually, despite having as many textual versions as alleged authors, it is easier to understand. Piers, a plain tiller of the soil, represents that socio-religious concept the Working Man – who during the course of a Plowman's lunch and twenty-nine pints at The Serf's Elbow treats us to a well-oiled panorama of medieval society. An opinionated witness from the start, he becomes more graphic if unreliable with every pint, till his final megalomaniac demise after pint twenty-nine. The poem, in the form of a dream, begins with the poet wandering into the garden in the middle of May, where the birds are singing, the flowers are blossoming and a total stranger is lying prostrate in a shallow ditch at the end of the garden. Upon revival, the poet asks the man to tell the story of how he came to be there, and Piers is roughly able to oblige.

It seems that around lunchtime of the day before,

Piers had forsaken the plough for the nearest inn. Amidst street cries – *'Every tenth bag, a free relic!'*, *'Hot Crosses!'* – Piers walks to an inn 'full of folk': merchants cheating at cards, lawyers twisting words, good-honest-working men, tinkers, cobblers, wastrels, pilgrims (*'When I was in. .'*), apprentices, two monks singing, 'Oh, Sir Jasper', cart menders (*'Y'big ends gone. Bouta'undred ducats. .'*), jesters, a Prioress sipping Pernod, a yeoman noshing hog-in-the-basket, and a Friar by the window in hunting boots, reading a dirty book and offering to absolve anything in a dress. Piers orders his usual bread, cheese and onions, all soaked in fennel, mace, cinnamon, saffron, ginger, cloves, aromatic root, thyme, garlic, majoram and pepper before sidling over to a cluster of villeins who all sidle a yard backwards as Piers gets stuck into his familiar stride, extracts of which, for the sake of convenience have been set into modern English prose.

' 'OW DO ALL! Ain't 'arf 'ot t'day. . .y'know oi till, reap, cut, mow, dig, manure, dibble, 'oe, plough, weed, lop an'top, thin out, prune, sow, 'arrow an' rake. . . . .FOR SIXPENCE A WEEK. . . .Oi kid you not. . .Na, it's gotta stop. . .an' 'is Lordship wiv 'is 'untin' mates, chargin' all over wot oi done, scarin' my 'orse shitless. . .Na, . . .bob a week or 'is 'arvest can rot. . .Oi'll go freelance oi will. . .cryin' out for men in Kent they are 'cos o' that Black Death. . .an' 'at's not just yer

gaffers neivver, eh?. . .Know wot oi mean, eh??. . .Fink oi
could do wivva 'oliday. . .might try anovver o' them package
pilgrimages. . .gotta few aches an' pains t'get rid of. . .AN' oi
need a couple of more teeth t' make up Goliath's bottom
jaw. . .psah, 'oly relics eh. . .mind, the wife'll 'ave t'go some
place else. . .she's tryin' t' get more pinches o'salt from Lot's
missus. . .still,. . . .'snot' at bad. . .Y' never know 'oo's gonna
be on the donkey in front, eh?. . Take last year. . .on the way
t' Lourdes, nice little French cricket ground. . .there's this bit
in front o'me. . .pin in the donkey's bum 'ad 'er right off 'er
path. . .well, 'ad t'elp 'er din oi?. . .Aw, dearie me. . .apple
wenches. . .stroll   on. . .an'   yer   know   wot   'ey
say 'bout 'em tours?. . .guaranteed no overtime in
Purgatory. . .well, it's me fifth trip now. . .this monk
reckoned oi'd go straight through. . . . . .'

After fifteen pints Piers flops down at a table and goes
into a deep sleep, during which various agencies debate
inside him e.g. Desire winks at Conscience but Alcohol
dissolves that idea; Power silences Hypocrisy; Prejudice
and Thirst, left unchallenged, re-awake Piers:

'Werza pap'r?. . .gotta see my stars. . .'ere we are. . .
Pisces. . .twentieth a lucky day for blood-lettin'. . .
yeah, fink oi'll get 'at done while th'ol sun's in Taurus. . .
wait a minute. . .moon's in Leo. 'at's not so good. . .
aw, sod it. . .Home Life livened up by a guest. . .
must be the wife's brother. . .twerp livens me up all right. . .
down from Oxford at fourteen wivva degree in magic an'
rhetoric. . .an' werz it got'im? bloody able-bodied beggar's
wot 'e is. . .wont' touch ale. . .only yer Malmsey for'im if yer
please. . .knows my job he says 'cos o' some Refill's
'Georgics'. . . Needs a good war 'e does. . .shudda bin wiv me
an' Lion'eart at 'Nople. . .all wogs an' sand an' blindin 'eat. . .
couldn't ride a camel meself. . .'ad t'be yer Seventh
Crossbows. . .an' wivva stint in th' ol' Twelth Hauberks. .Aw,
the times we thought we'ad Mustapha nailed. . .soldier of
Christ oi was. .an' now look at me. .th' only man in the country
'at does an 'onest day's work. . .tiller o'the soil?. .Oi'm the
bloody rudder o' the economy. .oi know the good life an' wot
the good Lord meant. . .Oi'm a worker o'Christ an'all. .fact
is, oi probably am Christ. .OI AM CHRIST. .OI AM
CHR. . . . .'

At this point, Piers has put away twenty-nine pints, so that although legless he is convinced of his divinity and carried to the nearest pond where, after all, he is unable to walk on the water. Many desperate strokes and seventeen hours later, he is brought round by the poet, who agrees that Piers should lead the Peasants' Revolt. 'Piers Plowman's' is a long, passionate, brilliant, persuasive and wonderful work which had no influence at all – except that Marxists generally allow English Literature to begin at this point.

By the time roods had finally given up, even moral tomes and histories of Britain were flourishing in special Mneumonic Couplets so that people could easily remember why to be patriotic and well-behaved. We call them 'Histories' when in truth they were florid narratives based on but in no way limited by facts, and the work of a new breed of men called Chroniclers (or journalists). They hailed from all over the country: Chris of Chester, Brian of Bath, Aubrey of Aldershot, Nicky of Bournemouth, Obsert atte Huddersfiield and so on. A similar outburst by Moralists produced 'The Owl and the Nightingale', a vicious debate on the ethics of nocturnal singing when other people are trying to get some sleep. 'The Ladder of Soap', 'The Ship of Longevity', 'The Ark of Shame' (very popular), 'Chastitie and the Pricke of Conscience' (remaindered), 'The Bridge of the House of Even More Shame' (film rights sold).

Meanwhile poets had fallen hopelessly in love with the Court's *joie de chivalrie*, gushing out unstoppable quantities of measured couplets. Few of their Romances have an ending – poets just couldn't bear to finish them. *Oh*, could the poet conjure a prettier damsel in worse distress, a bolder Knight, a wiser and lonelier hermit; *oh*, throw another tournament so as to list and describe everything for miles around; *oh*, set a new Love Problem to be analysed ad requiem in the hope of a mating in all positional variations. With the French as our tutors, Love now became a major sport of the utmost discretion to be played according to the Crafty Love Code.

Knight hears about or catches unforgettable sight of Someone Else's Wife, and immediately goes oxymoronic – freezing hot, hardly soft etc. When physically able loads up pigeon with the collected verse, stressing his frail condition, visions of her seething body and the chances of a talk about 'Us'. No sign of pigeon. No reply. 'Homme fatal' condition sets in. Bombards her with vows quilled in blood sachets of bitterest tears, handfuls of extracted hair, spends vigilant nights at the foot of a drainpipe awaiting orders. Ignored. Death closing in. Yet saved – by smile secreted in public place or deliberate drop of green handkerchief. Packs two horses for long weekend. Books French bed at Camelot. Presents himself to fashionable ironmonger for the latest accoutrements – fitted chainmail coat with matching metallic shoes, reflecting spurs, tinted visor, eight track stereo helmet, perfumed sword etc. Receives colour code or chooses one that suits him e.g. Pink Knight and invents mission e.g. to search out four-leafed clover. Promises fidelity and to send regular postcards.

It should not surprise the student that Knighthood, with all its high society, travel, gadgetry, illicit sex and plentiful violence, caught the popular imagination. Little boys didn't want to drive carts any more. Restless husbands from all levels of society were knocking together passable suits of armour and parading puzzled horses round to wives in the neighbourhood who really didn't know what on earth was going on.

Recognising this market, one of history's greatest opportunists, a Somerset restaurateur named Arthur King, bought up and tastefully converted an old castle at Camelot, where, by eating a certain number of good if rather pricey dinners prepared by his wife Ginny, all manner of man could be dubbed 'Sir', provided with a not very difficult little adventurette, and permitted to make themselves and their actions answerable to 'King' Arthur. However, when restaurant owners up and down the country started crowning themselves, things got a bit out of hand. Faced with a booming divorce rate and constitutional crisis, Romance Literature came to an end.*

It is now time to peruse the person of Geoffrey Chaucer (1340 – c.1440?) That we don't know enough about him means that anyone can have a go at inventing his life. And he was a genius – quite irresistible encouragement to litter his years with as many adversities, weaknesses and kinks as can plausibly be rumoured. But, let me say, they are unfounded: I could take Chaucer home to meet my parents.**

* Cf. 'Introduction Appliquée aux problèmes comparatifs d'une revue des réflexions évolutionnistes vers une science des genres gastronomiques' where French colleagues in 'scholarship nouveau' have done some excellent work on Arthur King – something which I have discreetly acknowledged in my hauntingly mellow translation of 'soi-distant' as 'King'.

** With one reservation, however. There is a soupçon of the Newt about Geoffrey, a certain dampness around the beard. I have seen some most unfair assumptions about the London Water Board, in attempts to explain the length of his slate at the Tabard Inn – not to mention a standing order with the Royal Pantry for a gallon of sack per day. It is odd that Geoffrey breathed his last shortly after this allowance was stopped. It is intriguing that he continued to write Romances until the moment an innkeeper called Harry told him to pack it in. On reflection I suppose the papering of his bedroom walls with wine labels might not just have indicated a desire to travel abroad. We may wonder whether the vintner's son who spent many years at an impressionable age watching gallons of canary being unloaded was as much interested – when it came to the spirit of the Renaissance – in Petrarch and Bocaccio as Grappa and Campari. Why was he prone to long, obscure digressions about necessity, medicine, dreams and stars? And those portraits of him! Paunched, a face fermenting with cuddly cynicism about the possible merits of treading the ground to which his eyes are invariably fixed, a rosary hung precariously in his amiably pickled fingers. This is one side of the great 'wet' or 'dry' debate which for years has been one of the most turbid and choppy backwaters of Chaucerian scholarship. In the exam I wouldn't give it much prominence. Better to settle on the day for a passing sentence, something like: 'Every fibre of his poetic being was soaked in the wine of courtly life, the tea of the ordinary man's existence, and the sack of his own average day'.

What Geoffrey actually did for English Literature is often obscured by posterity's conviction that he had read all those authors he mentions in his poems. For too long we have been reeling with the idea that Geoffrey must have woken up with Plato, analysed his dreams before breakfast, studied languages till opening time, lectured around lunchtime on astrology, relaxed with Boethius and theology till teatime, written something great as the queue built up for evening surgery, till at last he could retire with a little Froissart. But, for the sake of those who are determined to sleuth the labyrinths of Geoffrey's erudition, why not move in on . . .

Across

2. Holy caterer. Plenty for all if he starts.
5. Prehistoric serpent became Greek mathematician.
7. Phlemelanguineric. Get it?
9. There's a big one in Vienna (Good luck).

Down

1. A mountain, a good ship, now in the Louvre.
3. Wrinkled Lydian who found the price.
4. Reading this Roman tends to prolong life.
6. Saint who gets worse.
8. Illiad swash-buckler of the equestrian party.

10. Doesn't sound a happy king, but good with kids.
14. Roman emperor hopping around.
15. Saint in the summer converts last consonant.
16. Dream authority on Christian name terms with a tree.

11. Leaving Rome void.
12. Virtuoso musician AD64.
13. Who's that on the Ponte?

Chaucer's real achievements lie elsewhere. Possibly from listening to French sailors *en plein chanson* as they unloaded wine onto the wharves of his native Ipswich – or maybe not – Geoffrey somehow rumbled that the Normans had brought over . . . only what they wanted us to see. Hence his early life consisted almost entirely of drifting in and out of wangled jobs until close enough to Royal Ears to suggest that a British Literary Presence south-east of Dover was of the utmost importance.

His first trip was a great success. Through clandestine meetings with sympathetic poets in Italy, he got the details of Ottava Rima, and better still, information that a new French device, the Alexandrine, was remarkably similar. Back, in France everyone tried (in vain) to deceive him with Ballads and Lays till, following a break-in when he was almost caught copying them out, Geoffrey went on board at Calais clutching to him a set of brand new Alexandrines. On the road to London he dismantled them, and not being able to put them back together again, panicked, threw four feet out the window, made up a couple of rhymes, and presented to the King on his return at midnight, his own patent on Britain's finest verse vehicle to date: a decasyllabic Heroic Couplet. And he'd got the Ballads and Lays.

Months later, pigeons crossed in the post: the King was ordering him to test-write these new verse vehicles, as no-one had shown any sign of doing so. Geoffrey had no money. The King replied that he must start writing and to use the East Midlands dialect, as Wycliffe hadn't done too badly out of it.* Geoffrey at last agreed, complaining loudly that he didn't know what he ought to write about and would another trip abroad be all right? If staggering credit extended from a Florentine hostelry to one G. Chauceroni is as suspicious as it looks, our poet was there in the winter of 1386. Yet, again, he pulled it off, arriving back in London with a cloak stuffed full of Italian stories, plots and characters – and a considerable feeling of relief.

Geoffrey warmed up with a translation or two; and then took to commiserating with Harry at the Tabard about the mountain of time and the molehill of money involved in all this quillery. Harry paddled in his thoughts for a while. What arose between them late on that Tuesday afternoon in 1387 was nothing less than the outline of Geoffrey's greatest work. 'Let the market come to you then,' said Harry. 'And where do most people meet and get along together? In taverns and on holiday. So there's your maximum market. I know innkeepers all the way from here to, say, Canterbury. What you do is run tours from here to there and back, starting from outside the door. Group rates at the inns, no trouble. Sell the tours over the bar, throwing in a horse, overnight stops, all meals included and this is where your writing comes in – a story. You provide a story for each person to read out to the others on the way. A bit of fun for them and a souvenir. It'll while away the journey – because let's face it that stretch of road to Canterbury is not great to look at. Now, we get all sorts in here, so make up a good story for every type – you know, Millers, Friars, Merchants and that. All you have to do is to make them right, if you know what I mean. Spice the odd one up a bit, get a few having a

* An astute financial tip from the King this one – apart from being the only dialect he and his friends understood. In fact, this is one of Geoffrey's other great breakthroughs: we can also understand what he's saying – just about – which is more than can be said for Ezra £'s versions of Chaucer in modern US/Cantonese. 'Parlement of Foules' is not quite 'Chicks in the Commons'.

go at one another, but don't go mad. We don't want any trouble – and we don't want any Prioress having to read out more of what your Miller likes to hear. Get your copies done, and we're away. It's publicity for you, and regular ducats. Whenever you like, collect your stories up and publish them. You'll make a powder keg! And, mark my words, you'll be doing a good job. You won't be writing about foreign nobs or old tribes, you'll be writing about us. Now, is it a deal?' 'Yes', whimpered Geoffrey.

Of Anglo-Saxon literature, hardly anything remains; with Norman literature virtually nothing gets finished. Therefore Geoffrey finally falls into the Norman tradition as 'The Canterbury Trails' were never actually finished. Yet in a comparatively short space, he showed us ourselves in our own language. What could be more British than telling stories at each other's expense on horseback? That he created characters is clear from the way we discuss them as if they were real people, invisibly riding off the pages up our driveways. When Geoffrey died, the crowds carried his coffin to Westminster Abbey, and little children cried in the streets. Carved on his tomb, his own epitaph:

> 'Sothely for to seyn withoute more delay,
> As I wol yow seyn, ther nis namore to seye.'

Explicit Secunda Pars

The Metal Age

The study of fifteenth-century Literature has about it one disturbingly central fact: there wasn't any. Well, not much. There was Malory, who'd turned himself over to yet another conceptual washing of Camelot's linen; Mandeville jumping on the travel bandwagon with a pot-boiling 'Europe on Five Saints a Day'; and a cure for insomnia called Lydgate, who single-handedly obliged apothecaries to accept a lower standard of living. In short, anything any good was immediately assumed to have been left behind by Geoffrey. So far ahead was he in fact that he'd effectively pulled the plug on British inkwells for the next hundred and fifty years – a gap to which people react differently. Some panic, and start claiming wildly that Lydgate and co. were terrific, wouldn't read anything else etc.; others refer to it variously as an Age of Literary Innocence, a dry century, age of transition etc. while here at Pidgin College we generally refer to it as The Metal Age of English Literature.

One of the difficulties for Literature was that patrons weren't interested in it. They had wars to wage, deals to push through. Yet, ironically, or perhaps logically, the chief event in Prose was the correspondence that passed through several generations of the Paston family in Norfolk. At least they never intended the letters to be published – any more than the Forsytes expected to be on television. A letter might indicate what Literature was up against.

To my right worshipful husband, John Paston, be this delivered in haste.

Right reverend husband, I recommend me to you. As for gathering of money I saw never a worse season. Thrice over have I counted the coffers since Wednesday last and seen, I trow, for the reformation of our costs. It is not needful of yet to mortgage the hens.

Item, my Lord of Moreland has a company of brothel with him that reck not what they do, and such are most for to dread. Good numbers of our fellowship passed to God on Tuesday upon a riot at Yarmouth. His Lordship smote off the leg of your beadsman Dick with twenty-eight strokes of a rusty sword. May he be set fast in the stocks and pelted with filth. Dick of late eschews boisterousness, and is well amending though not so whole as he was.

Item, it has fallen to me in recent times to overhear the names Caxton, Columbus, Joan of Arc and Constantinople. I wot not, if these be newly recruited to Lord Moreland's mischief; or those that ye owe money to. Thus far have they not vexed us in any wise.

36

Item, Sharp told me of a farmer that prayeth you will vouch-safe to let him buy of your farm barley. I ventured 400 crowns for an hundred weight, whereupon his door appeared with noise in front of my gaze. From a high window he commanded me that I should go home, for other answer could I have none. God for His holy mercy give grace that he will pay when his ears are nailed to his cartwheel next week.

Item, my Lord Scales will know the disposition of Thomas Pryce to his daughter Jane. Already five and thirty years on his hands, her father has sore set his purse on the match and she, following the common voice, rages to be ravished in any wise.

Item, twelve bordered pastries, four sauced capons and a cart of salt, containing therein a statue of wax of yourself are near to being conveyed to my Lady of Bentworth, the which I hope she will receive in good part. Chancery may not sit unto the time there be a new Sheriff, set by her husband.

Item, the monks of Ely set up a right good market this Sunday last. I took me from there with diverse girdles, powder boxes and such swingeing wine as set Master Dick full on song. Much more would I write to you, but I lack leisure and now must fetch more straw for the servants. Written at Little Snoring in great haste the Saturday next after St. Bartholomew's Eve as light faileth and Mistress Scrope now asketh 6d. for a candle. God help you,

Yours,
Margaret Paston

As Margaret's interest in books goes little beyond their efficacy in propping up table legs or holding doors open, any recognition of authors is liable to be out of the question – unless, of course, they owe her the folding stuff. Perhaps Oscar is right on this one: 'It is only by not paying one's bills that one can hope to live in the memory of the commercial classes'. None the less, patrons ignoring authors was only one way of our losing them. Judging from the frailty of law and order in Margaret's world more than a few might have perished from sudden over-attention.

Still whatever the reasons, there came a time when we could no longer avoid the truth that England had no notable Poets or Prosicians. So we did the only thing possible: we left Literature to the populace. As, by and large, they couldn't read or write this led to singing, with village folk strumming their ballads or roaring their carols not knowing that someone would eventually bother to write it all down; nor that their efforts would induce such prim delight at Merrie England sherry evenings; nor even less that we would have among us people whose carrot juice would be spluttered all over their committed beards if you dared to suggest that something arising from community living, especially working-class community living, was not worth keeping. You will even find the more remote the region, the more utterly incomprehensible the dialect, the more a ballad is cherished – and as often as not perpetrated by roods who had taken their final refuge in border areas, or elderly Newts who had retreated in complete disarray to such far-flung places as the western shores of Ireland. At this juncture the collection of ballads possessed by a junior colleague of mine, Dr. Stephen Cherrytree, puts me in mind of his particular favourite which he both sings with penetrating guile and hangs tastefully above his astrological almanac of Morris Dancing lying in a late Ming fruit-bowl. It is called 'Th' Laird o' Geordie':

> As ae wa'oot scrungin'
> Sing cuccu, nu!
> Merie sing, cuccu!
> O aye wi'yon prinkle snipsy
> Sing ninny, nu!
> Noddy, ninny nu!
>
> By yocked th'laird o' Geordie
> Sing riddle diddle!
> Riddle diddle doo!
> An' whusked muh lass awa'
> Sing fiddle faddle!
> Fiddle faddle foo!

Usually a ballad was passed orally as a result of normal gregariousness, so it had about as much chance of remaining in its original form as a harmless rumour. Of British balladeers none is so well known as Blind Roger with his seismographic ears and elephantine memory.

When he died locals reckoned he'd taken about two hundred ballads with him. No comment.* Yet if Blind Roger were alive today we'd probably see him taking part in that phase of youth's spiritual circuit-training which requires it to take up a guitar and rucksack and lie across three seats on the benches of transport terminii ('I've crashed' is apparently adequate explanation of this behaviour) or sit crosslegged on highways seriously expecting to be allowed into other peoples' cars. Still, he's not here so let us return to the ballad which we may define as a bumpkin's epic of metricised gossip.

There were also ballads, called carols, which were sung out at Christmas time. The earliest carols betray the sort of dim apprehension of the Christian story which finally forced clerics to put it in pictures on their church windows. In this very early version – at least to the tune of 'O Little Town of Bethlehem' – we see the medieval village minstrel vigorously embracing the Nativity story, but still not getting it quite right:

> O Joseph dear it's not my clothes,
> You see I'm great with child –
> Just what the hell am I to suppose?
> Now Joseph don't go wild.
>
> I can explain if you'll shut up,
> The baby's due tomorrow.
> Some friends are coming round to sup
> In a stable we can borrow.
>
> Shepherds and wise men numbered six
> And found Joseph waiting for them –
> So which one of you clever dicks
> Wants his face through the floor then?
>
> Poor Gabriel arrived too late
> With words from the Almighty –
> Six guests lay round about prostrate
> Not one had brought a nightie.

---

* However, neither roods nor Newts should be credited with inventing the ballad stanza. We owe that to the verbal forms used among Hittite drovers.

This erroneous carol was just one of many which showed that people simply weren't learning enough in Church. So priests to liven things up a bit, started to clown about in the services. This is how Drama began. And why it ended. Priests became a trifle too Thespian.

Although the Church then promptly banned its own invention, the days of jamboree preaching had left their mark. All the enraged dancers, jugglers, minstrels and acrobats who'd lost their audiences to performing clergymen were getting ready to do their own plays.

Unable to ignore this, the Church continued to be odd about Drama. It now condemned the souls of all Players as men of the Devil, vagabonds, urchins and poofs whilst manipulating guildsmen to stage Bible stories – enacted, of course, by the very same vagabonds, urchins and poofs. This unreliable element is no doubt the explanation for those incidents in our early Drama that were not very Christian. . . .

40

Plays were put on in towns through the year at religious peaks i.e. people had the day off. A horse drew a wheeled platform (the stage) round to the various popular and crowded areas of the town. This was good business for the guild with the right play in the right place. The Master Bakers, for example, were rather sensitive about their mission to stage the Crucifixion. Only a lunatic – for a short while – would have stood in the way of the Light Weaponry Guild's feelings about David and Goliath. Nor was there much arguing the toss with the Clothiers Guild about Jacob. But that wasn't the end of it; because each guild then wanted to see its message going across in the main squares at their busiest hours, leading to some of the most unholy scrambles to get there first. Cart axles were sawn through, roads blocked, ale poisoned. And any victor was immediately subject to reprisals during the performance. This usually took the form of heckling or rigged punch-ups, except for the notorious instance of a horse taking off in mid-play to sort out a really voluptuous mare who just happened to appear on the far side of the market place. Is it any wonder that these plays soon earned the nicknames of Miracle or Mystery Plays? It was a miracle if any of them arrived. And reduced to a total mystery if ever one did.

By the time that Drama had established itself it had come to mean, at the very least, breach of the peace. The civic and religious bodies who'd survived grew apprehensive: the genre had to be made less dangerous. So it was decided that plays were now to be acted on separate days, and to stress in their content, with visions of the Eternal Bonfire, what God would do to you if you didn't behave yourself. Law and order was restored fairly easily, but then alas the concept of good behaviour got quite out of hand. Plays were actually written with a hero called Good Deeds, He, of course, always triumphed on the Day of Judgement over far more important things like Women, Drinking and Property which were shown to be treacherous pieces of worldly rubbish. And all Man ever does about this is look pathetic, till Good Deeds leads him off to Heaven. As students sometimes find this state of affairs hard to believe, some extracts follow from 'Anyone':

'Anyone'

Solidarity, renegotiations, fish & chips,
a nice hot cup of tea, dirty jokes and
winning the pools

ALL: Ecky thump! Right fookin' party in 'ere lads.

A: Hello there. Can I have a chip?

ALL: Tha' can 'ave nobbut t'paper.

A: Go on. Let's have the smallest, greasiest one you've got.

ALL: Nay. If us give thee one, 'appen as 'ow th'all be wantin' 'em all.

A: That's not so.

ALL: And it is yer daft pillock.

Exit SOLIDARITY etc.

Fast cart' sex before marriage
Getting rich very quickly

ALL: I'd like to stay with you. You're a really nice guy. I mean it, seriously. But I've got to see a man about a dog.

A: Can't you take me with you – or come along for just a short while?

ALL: Make up your mind, sunshine. Can't be in two places at once. 'Bye now.   *Exit* FAST CART etc.

Wife' old slippers' clean sheets
Holiday with the kids, meals on time

ALL: Hello darling. I've brought you some sand-wiches. Lettuce, your favourite. The kids have been asking where you were. I told them to get on and eat their meal. I got a full refund from the Broads – after an argument of course.

A: Can't you stay for a cuddle? Tell me how John's archery's getting on.

ALL: Well, I would darling but the butcher's dropping round a hog's head this afternoon. Oh, and there's the milkman to settle with. I'll give your love to the kids. There'll be something ready for you on the table when you get back. See you later, then. Have a good day.   *Exit* WIFE etc.

Scoring a goal, backhander down the
line, tremendous sprint at the end,
taking the off stump with one that
moved late

A: Thank God you're here. You cheer me up no end. I've often played you back through my mind's eye and wondered how it must have looked to the others when I did it.

ALL: Did what?

A: You know. All those brilliant flukes.

ALL: We are only memories. We stay for the split second you had us and then go.

Exit SCORING A GOAL etc.

43

(ANYONE, alone, sniffs armpits, breathes determinedly into cupped hand in front of mouth and sniffs again. Turns to audience.)

A: Well, it isn't me. Can't understand it.

(Enter, GOOD DEEDS to tumultuous applause. Enter DEATH to hysterical booing. ANYONE bounds up to GOOD DEEDS like playful dog, receives lecture, is lead away like myopic spaniel. DEATH swears appalling oath many times. Bursts into tears. Curtain.)

Even with the laziest, most penniless illiterates Drama couldn't fail – because it landed on peoples' doorsteps, free of charge, in spoken English. However, the popularity of Drama, which encouraged people to think that reading wasn't necessary, very nearly persuaded William Caxton to stay in Belguim. Why he ever wanted to go to Belgium in the first place is still a mystery. Why does anyone go to Belgium? However, it seems that William, whose livelihood depended on a bit of this and that here and there one way or another, had heard that there was now Literature in England which could, profitably, be printed. William's first action, after setting up his Press at Westminster, was an economic measure: the dropping of the final 'e' on as many words as possible. Fortunately, William did have some aesthetics otherwise I feel we might have lost a lot more letters, particularly the way g's and z's just guzzle up the ink – not to mention having to pay a fortune to your best workmen before they'd even look at those bends. Still, William's first monetary crisis came when he ran out of English Literature far earlier than he'd been led to believe. Naturally, Geoffrey was top of the queue and had made him a fair bit, and he hadn't done too badly out of Wycliffe, but the prospect of trying to flog Lydgate drove him into translations of foreign works for the rest of his life.

But we should not underestimate William Caxton's achievement in such a short time. He obliged more schools to teach people how to read – which is something only crypto-Fascist reactionaries still seem to find quite a good idea. And reading was something to be learnt when spelling was on a do-it-yourself basis, grammar didn't exist and punctuation was an affair of mood. Aloft must William be held, though, for providing writers with an exciting new incentive. They were able to say that their books had 'gon to press(e)', whence they would return 'in print(e)' to be admired throughout the realm. Doubtless this is why we got some Literature out of the next century.

It's certainly why we got John Skelton. Only the advent of printing could explain his behaviour – although he was a vicar and this was a very good century for vicars. His first book excited him to confess that he was Poet Laureate. His next book took up the subject of John Skelton and unashamedly climaxed with his coronation. Whereas medievals wriggled in unworthiness when they wrote, and were often too shy to put their names on manuscripts, Rev. Skelton began a manuscript with a whole volley of signatures, through the middle of which ran a thin streak of the fastest verse on earth. He just couldn't wait to get to press. Even his mournful poems get you from 0 – 60 words in two seconds. Yet he could hardly blame lack of free time for his apparent wish to get writing over with as quickly as possible. Anyone who was a tutor to Henry VIII quite clearly would have seen little of his pupil during the day, and nothing of him at night. Personally I don't think Henry ever rolled up. Did someone with six wives, umpteen executions and a Reformation, seriously have a Catholic priest as his tutor? So, instead, our Poet Laureate moaned that any shortcomings in his own verse were due to the state of the language. But then he won't be the first brother of the quill to shove out the 'give us the tools' argument after completing a work that looks more than usually mortal.

Talking of death, Skelton's is an interesting one. He arrived at Westminster in his pyjamas the night before he died, so that he could be buried there. Or, at least, that's what he said. The small matter of Cardinal Wolsey being in the mood to break all ten commandments at once, because he'd got hold of Skelton's poem about him was, of course, nothing to do with it. However, Nature took its course unaccelerated and early in the sixteenth century the Charlie Chaplin of English Letters passed away. But the end of that fatal poem is still with us, as Helter-Skeltonic as tomorrow:

My name is John Skelton
Knees, never knelt on,
Should now be dwelt on
As we pelt on
Over pons asinorum
To the crux criticorum –
Wolsey's a cockalorum!
Fit for the jug
From his mother's dug –
A cardinal thug!
While I am Rector of Diss
With nothing remiss
Except that I
Feeling fly
Wrote this!

William in the Wings

There is a good deal of alarmist talk about the sixteenth century – for which I personally blame the Renaissance. To speak of 'complex and dynamic new forces' is sheer panic mongering, insanely over-complicated and, actually, morally reprehensible. A candidate either experiences frisbee for the rest of term in a condition of strange, barefoot hilarity; or, like a lemming, drops into the dungeons of a serious library never to return, until next of kin – called to identify the body when the notes have been cleared away – finds that the poor devil has strayed hopelessly far away from the Penguin Classics in translation. The Renaissance, then, can be terminal. But taken sensibly – a small Giotto downstairs, perhaps a page of Erasmus now and again in mixed company, or a sympathetic perusal of Leonardo's plans for Concorde – it can be a very useful movement to explain away any event between 1450–1650 for which there seems to be no other cause.

I suppose it is as well to say early on that the real key to the century is neither the Renaissance (see above) nor the Reformation (see below). That position belongs to Women. Remove them, and you will be left with hardly any Sonnets, no Reformation, four British thrones empty

– and a fifth if you don't think Henry could have survived. We shall, however, begin with a penetrating study of the Reformation, itself something of a study in penetration if a scholar can be frank.

The Reformation, a marriage guidance and furniture removal service set up by His Royal Heaviness, confused the Church for the rest of the century. Prose was given a singularly rough time by the men of God who got it smuggled, banned, accepted, banned again and burnt again as they fought to decide which of the Reformation's three causes – Henry's pocket, Henry's stomach and Henry's codpiece – was most central to religious belief. Hot from his recent success in blowing all his father's money, H. felt it was only the Church's duty to let him have a go at spending all theirs, even if the Protestant rebels had already enlisted his sympathy by making the Eucharist into a three-course meal. A Welsh ambassador dolefully records Henry's wish to see 'a chicken in every church'. But the main reason (frankly speaking) was further down the body monarchic. Harry's reptilian gaze had fastened upon nimble-thighed Anne Boleyn. His continental wife, Catherine, had dragged Henry over new frontiers of boredom long ago. So when the Pope refused to uphold Spanish soap and Paella as suitable grounds for divorce, Henry, despairing of understanding Italians, broke with Rome.

Now that Henry had found his way to Anne Boleyn everyone else had to find their own way to God, so Bill Tyndale quickly found his way to The Translator's Head for a working lunch. 'Your man in the street is going to need a Bible he can understand – and fast!', confided Bill beneath the Wycliffe portrait in the backroom, yet within earshot of a Mr. Coverdale, already pensively thumbing his way through the Highway Code's sales figures and shortly to depart with the speed of a greased weasel. Two weeks later Bill's version was ready, as was Mr. Coverdale's. However death was around the corner, as Bill had allowed a certain degree of colloquial levity to creep into his style, no doubt the result of thinking he was onto a good thing. Mr. Coverdale, by association, was also returned to the loam. For it was on the morning that Henry didn't stay in bed, rolling instead towards chapel to brush up his Latin, only to discover this sort of thing:

'Baptism' (Coverdale)
'Quick dip' (Tyndale)

'Shrove Tuesday' (Coverdale)
'Pancake Day' (Tyndale)

'I AM THAT I AM' (Coverdale)
'It's me' (Tyndale)

'In my Father's house are many mansions' (Coverdale)
'The old man's not short of space' (Tyndale)

that both authors had been boiled in acid, strangled, garrotted, burnt, exhumed and jumped upon by mid-afternoon.

With publicity like that available, publishers flooded the market with Bibles of all sorts. And with Tudor Church policy continuing to arrive more or less over-night, lucrative purges could be guaranteed. But before long there were simply too many Bibles on sale, added to which the weak and often dead link in the venture – the translator – could no longer afford the overheads of frantic disguise, late-booking fees and enforced exile, out of the diminished profits. Thenceforth, any religious Prose in book form had to be like Parson Hooker's 'Laws of Elastic Policy' which flexed a gentle logice over all sides of the fence at once.

It was now that the Pamphlet came of age, mainly because the penalty tended to be the hand rather than the head, though, depending on the monarch, this might be accompanied by a little playful removal of the finger-nails or curiosity at how far the human thumb can be stretched. By its argumentative, anonymous and non-profit-making nature, the Pamphlet attracted all hues of crackpot. The Puritans were the most fertile loonies. Even the arrival of the potato detonated Josiah Watson, who, ignoring the royal passion for chips, wouldn't have sported much below the elbow after this little outburst:

49

For the love of CHRIST are we all gone BLIND to the UNPARDONABLE SIZE of Teuton's Princes? Swell they not daily with the ague of KARTOFFELN, spread to their very cakes? And ha'we not legions of EYES AND BALLS rolling in the SWAMPS OF LUST without lascivious munching of the SWEET POTATO? Do honest Meat and fair Vegetables need truck with the Ornament of a Potato? What hey! Hey, hey!! Hey, Hey, Hey!! No more need we that Potato race of Bishops in their LEWD, FANTASTICAL JACKETS! Fried? Mashed? Roasted? Done with a delicious curry sauce? Tis all divers Wiles of the Devil to dish up the LOATHSOME VEGETABLE OF ANTICHRIST, swollen in the filthy Charnel House of the Clod, the cause of such hideous SCOFFING as will surely drown us all in the Stinking Whirlpool of the Tiber, wherein is dumped all the noisome shit from the bowels of the land of Machiavel –!–? POTATO. O! O! O? Tis a pretty way to end a word –AN WE WERE IN ROME OR SWANSEA. Means it perchance that British kitchens are to be laid open for the entire DUNGHILL of PAPIST PASTA? Shall our children suffer the Whore's pox of Tortellini? Shall we all slither down the sluice gates to Gomorrha on a plate of Ravioli al Duomo?? Rather a mouthful of Fettucini with the Devil. Calvary were only fit place to kill our Lord AN'T WERE A POTATO PATCH . . .!

Fortunately, the Renaissance was producing a new type of man – who generously thought of himself as the greatest thing since gunpowder. This was the Ideal Gentleman.

He is from a good family – the sort who actually don't mind if the Queen and her train descend on them at the slightest notice, clean out the larder, drain the cellars and push off again without offering a penny. He's a scholar, a poet, a linguist, a man who can fence any foreigner into a corner or spot a Sou' Wester through the tang in the breeze. He has come to the Court of Queen Elizabeth hoping to wangle a cushy job. His clothing will suggest a comprehensive personality, effeminately virile from the tip of his twee beard to the chiselled muscles of his calves: in fact, there was no point coming to Court if you didn't have good legs. Any religious leanings will, understandably, be towards himself. For the following image of the Renaissance Court Favourite (overleaf) we are indebted to the depths of Pidgin College Library where an old Chapbook of social types was recently discovered. Controversy rages around who he actually is. I consider we are looking at Toadingham, Crawleigh or Leighton Buzzard.

A: The Laws of Commercial Shipping by J. Drake, a thin volume. More important is what's hidden behind it: The Blue Wines of Italy, Cesare Borgia's mouth-foaming guide to entertaining awkward people.

B: Favourite's Year Book. Essential reading. Tables based on the Queen's features reveal that Toadingham is on the way out having collected an awful 70% of the Royal frowns dispensed. Crawleigh, however, is currently basking in 68% of the Royal smiles. Dorset and Birmingham making a late challenge with some tasteful compliments and running well until both, unfortunately, threw invitation cloaks into the same puddle.

C: 'Say it Again, Cicero' and Euphues Made Simple just about black out 'One in the Codpiece' by N. Macchiavelli, a young Florentine's view of success. So virtuous is power that you shouldn't be too bothered how you get it.

D: Drake casual, listening fingers round a New World timber stem and secrete noiseless little jets of Frobisher Flake, the Queen's blend. Never forget Her Majesty once flung out Toadingham for making unseemly gurgling noises with his pipe; nor the effect of hot cinders on a rival's tights.

E: Beard. Indicates age and protein intake. Control the sea dog suggestion otherwise you might find yourself with an unwanted naval command and Her Majesty merrily waving goodbye to you at Tilbury.

F: Codpiece. A bit of fun besides being your security against undisciplined games of croquet, short fencing partners and early season looseners on the bowling green.

G: Dagger. by Stiletto of Milano. 'The Diplomat's Choice.' One in the Codpiece contains a list of vital points where such intervention is liable to settle things with a minimum of fuss.

H: Court Creepers. Splayed design muffles noise. Especially suitable for little journeys at night when travelling on business with F or G.

52

Poetry was composed for us by these Gentlemen. There is presumably some lost agreement whereby they would only write about two subjects. Their first subject we might just about call a Pastoral Subject. 'Just about' because handsome, deodorised shepherds with degrees in Moral Philosophy wandering around meadows full of beautiful people with Greco-Roman names eating ambrosia in diaphonous smocks who all proceed to fall utterly in love with the wrong person immediately, splash around in rivers of milk, twine flowers lyrically into a neighbour's hair, dance with the sheep, carve poems on tree-trunks, drape themselves inquisitively round dahlias etc. until a total stranger drops from the sky with an antidote to this hallucogen whereupon it's all pardons and a general clear-up, is not exactly your average day in the countryside. But for the Gentlemen, weary of bomb plots and Court intrigues, a little shepherderie in Cloud Cuckoo Land was the perfect break.

However, if you don't believe what they wrote about their holidays then you're not likely to swallow what they said about their second subject-girlfriends.* Somehow or other they were all going out with married women of the nobility to whom they'd given a classical codename. This, in fact, was wise because when you dedicated your 'Sonnets to Daffodel' to her great and powerful husband, whose pipe you were not fit to empty etc., it was better not to stress that Daffodel was his wife. Yet somehow all these ladies looked exactly the same, possessed the same magical properties, behaved identically and were all supposed to be unique. These Gentlemen would have us believe that flowers wouldn't blossom, the sun wouldn't come out, Spring itself wouldn't arrive until hordes of cherry-lipped, pearl-toothed, lily-and-roses faced, sapphire-eyed blondes from all over central London decided to smile. Should we really believe them? After all, they did make out that Elizabeth I was a glorious blonde, a regular cod-piece cracker – when, despite all the pearls and butterfly suits, she was only about sixty, approximately toothless and capable of going through a pipe or down a pint faster than Falstaff.

A meeting with the Gentlemen is overdue, so we shall take a quick look at two Sirs, one Earl and a top Secretary.

Enter, first of all, Wyatt and Surrey whose main importance is tht they gave Shakespeare the idea of

* I have a student called Jack whom I have heard, but not seen, for the last three weeks. At least, I think it is his megaphone outside my seminars which are apparently on 'bourgeois week-end papier-mâché shepherds' and apparently totally illegal until such time as the Faculty should take a referendum on Elizabethan pay policy 1579–1603, whose outcome he is trying to sway by calling for a return to the spirit of Tamburlaine among local agricultural workers.

Rosencrantz and Guildenstern. They were called in to help Henry, who couldn't get to sleep after lunch for the thought that there hadn't been enough Literature during his reign. So they, in the best traditions of Geoffrey, rooted the Sonnet out of Italy and planted it in England. Henry, relieved, told them to get writing. And it's at this point that the strain of being the first Ideal Gentlemen and handling a new Poetic Vehicle told on the judgement of the two men. Wyatt addressed his Sonnets to Anne Boleyn – and, for his trouble, the rest of his living gaze to the interior brickwork of the Tower. Surrey, eager to atone for this blot, donated blank verse around a theme entitled 'Miscellaneous Totty'. Better tactics you might think if Surrey had first of all looked over Rex v. Tyndale & Coverdale to discover Henry's taste for inclusive executions. And so it happened that when Catherine's turn came for the mental headshake, Henry was loath to neglect her relative and duly lopped Surrey's top for him as well.

By Elizabethan times, the Ideal Gentlemen were organised. The image, Sir Philip Sidney created for himself was nothing short of a new concept in maturity: eager pursuit of virtue, constructive use of leisure, plenty of fresh fruit, always doing the decent thing etc. Spencer, a Secretary was bowled over by him. There's little doubt about the identity of the unusual Pale Gentleman who recurs flippantly throughout 'The Faerie Queene'. There's no doubt at all that he's the 'Philophyll' of the Sonnets. But whether Sir Philip's influence on Edmund was a good thing or not is doubtful. Has anyone survived a reading of 'The Faerie Queene'? Edmund did seem to panic a bit, as if he was being watched. He starts off by telling you it's an epic – the author's way of letting you know he's taking the whole thing bloody seriously – something which immediately induces a sense of fear in the reader because it's going to be long, heavy and probably unfinished. There's going to be a huge design with an earth-shrinking purpose, enormous characters lumbering through a monolithic story. Well, Edmund didn't quite do that. As far as anyone's been able to find out there isn't a story. He just used every technique to date on all the subjects he'd ever heard of, and sprinkled the whole lot with 'Poesy'. The result was not unlike large chunks of Turkish delight, a load of sweet, powdered stodge about Wonderfulness, Preciousness, History and the kitchen sink. The problem – everyone felt – was to say what it was about because they were all proud he'd done it. It was the biggest poem since Geoffrey. Ben Jonson, a bricklayer, didn't have a clue what was going on 'He writ no language. A coupla weeks on the site would 'ave 'im straight.'

Alas, Ben's dusty, concrete finger could be pointed at all the Ideal Gentlemen, who had created such a craze for Quillery that authorship was positively expected to occur in a Gentleman as a type of secondary social characteristic. There was the coming-out Sonnet to Chloris, after which you were supposed to ransack mythology and botany to describe her. Even though their love poetry would induce an aimless drowsiness in the most ardent sex maniac, fourteen lines three times a week was the agreed minimum.* These 275,000 Sonnets, none of which spring to mind, did at least warm up the Sonnet Vehicle for its most memorable driver.

* Jack continues to come over loud and clear. It seems the Chancellor's life is in some danger as the sudden fashion for Sonnet writing was really the work of 'Cardboard Monarchists' out to create a thoroughly erotic atmosphere in which the virgin Queen might be persuaded to go all the way. Jack has apparently given the Chancellor a deadline for the removal of all Sonnets from the curriculum. This demand was re-affirmed at his vodka and crackers party given on the eve of an anti-Kipling rally in Luton.

And now the time is ripe for the story of William Shakespeare. However, as the story of William Shakespeare is also rather ripe, we shall convey it in two parts.

Part One

'The Pride of Warwickshire' (Certificate U)

Once upon a time during the reign of Good Queen Bess when Englishmen ruled the seas and folk shouted 'Hurrah!' through the streets, there lived a young couple who had settled in the little town of Stratford-on-Avon to share their lives together. So dearly did they love their cosy, half-timbered cottage in the high street where the gabled roofs rang daily with the cries of children rushing pell-mell out of sunlit orchards to the fair on the village green, that it seemed their happiness couldn't be more complete. Yet they longed, above all, for just one thing – the birth of a baby boy. With time, that blessing was theirs. One bright April morning John hurried home from the Town Hall to find Mary sobbing tears of joy. 'What is it dearest?', he entreated. 'I've had Shakespeare,' she said.

William grew to be a lively lad, full of fun and mischief, and always writing. He went to the local grammar school, one of the best in the world, and would have pryed more deeply into the lore of bygone ages had not Fate decreed otherwise, so that he had to get a local job. Some say he was apprenticed to a local butcher and certainly there was no finer preparation for Elizabethan Tragedy. Soon he married a local girl and she provided him with three local children. But by now the lure of the stage was strongly upon him, and so he left Stratford and went to win his way in London. He didn't take Anne and the babes with him because he feared for their safety in the life of the big city. But he came home time and time again – in the end a wealthy and successful father who could buy a fine house for his loved ones. He lived out the twilight where he had known the dawn of

57

his years and since 1616 has slept peacefully in the local churchyard.

Whereas Part 1 is for all parents and children who can fit the Stratford run into a day – 'Before we go inside you put that penknife AWAY'; 'Not AT the swans, Peter'; 'DID you put jam on this gentleman's chair?'; 'Half of them in the hall, I think, and the rest over the fireplace' – Part 2 of the Shakesapeare story deals with a genius on the loose in London, and therefore contains material which may be considered offensive. If you have a child who should on no account be introduced to this material, then you have one similar to Marmaduke, my eldest. I found that with him, after tucking him up tightly, a very slow reading of Part 1 with a light orchestra in the background had him flat out by the fifth sentence, so if it works for twenty-eight year olds you should be safe with anyone younger. I had thought to take a razor to Part Two and lob it onto a high shelf, but Marmaduke climbs well so I tend to favour the first method.

Part Two

'Call Me Willy' (Certificate X)

To get on with his writing was not William's first intention when he came to London. First of all, he had to sort out an urgent personal problem. While you and I know, on balance, whether we're the Archbishop of Canterbury or not, Shakespeare for some reason didn't know who he was. Hours of trying out spellings of his name in different handwritings had led him to believe that he was more or less Shakespeare, Shaksper, Shahspear or at least someone like that, but then he would fall back with a puzzled groan: was he Bacon after all? What about the Earl of Oxford? Maybe Ben was right and he was the Swan of Avon, whatever that meant. This identity crisis took William to the Mermaid Tavern more and more often and thence into a pinball of relationships

hoping for an answer. One hundred and fifty-four Sonnets were the result of two friendships he made where scholars have been quick to point out how the outside numbers symbolically add up to the inside one or conversely when subtracted leave nothing. It makes you think. But then Shakespeare is always getting up to strangely meaningful things like that. Would it give you comic relief to pluck an old friend's skull out of the earth and prance all over a graveyard asking him where the rest of him was?

A long summer of tossing the sugar cane and other sporting achievements more Greek than British was only marred by the arrival of the Fiend. She was ugly, sexy and treacherous, but William fell for her against all his better nature. Every Thursday at four o'clock he'd traipse round to the back of the Globe not knowing any poetic reason for being there, so he'd end up writing something about Time which you could always say something impressive about. One Thursday she wasn't there, but lying in the grass was a note. She had gone off with Laddy after hearing some wench swooning in the Mermaid about how he was the only begetter worth the distance. William felt crushed, hopeless, What gratitude! He'd only immortalised them in verse! And he didn't even get their names – or his own for that matter. From then on, as Ben tells us, William hugged life's shores, only occasionally pushing the boat out for 'small Latins and a few Greeks'.

Within weeks the Sonnets had all sold out. William had put Drama into Poetry and the deposit down on his first town house. Now he was poised to put Poetry into Drama and pack the theatres. No sculptors or painters had realised there was a public out there with money in its pockets crying out for products of the Renaissance. William's Midas touch told him there was a Golden Age just round the corner. What was the chap's name in the Mermaid last week? Kept Hiccupping. Sounded like Urbage. Must ask Ben.

The Golden Trade

'**B**loody pre-Shakespearean Drama!' screamed Henslowe, smashing an abacus up and down in an otherwise quiet corner of The Mermaid. 'Couldn't feed a cat on it!' he soliloquised. Ben ignored him, halfway through his seventh attempt that morning in his best Latin to turn a London brick into a gold bar. Outside Burbage noisily experienced a tragic emotion against a drainpipe.

'Is there a Mr. Henslowe here please?'

Henslowe returned a rather shaken abacus to its place on top of the account books, and resumed a more or less natural colour.

'Yes, I'm Philip Henslowe. And who are you?'

'William Shakespeare.'

'Oh, not again! I've had three of you this morning.'

'Well, there's only one of me, you big theatre manager.'

'That's what they all said. So I'll say to you what I said to all the others. The Queen wants a play by tomorrow, which'll then go on at The Swan for two afternoons. Whatever anyone else wants, I want two hours of stab-you-in-the-balls-Italy but no knocking the Tudors, a sub-plot, twelve bodies at the end, messengers, clowns, a

61

ghost, a Fool, dirty jokes and great poetry. There's ten quid in it for you. No blank verse plumbing mind, you great poetry, O.K.? Oh, and you have to act three parts in your play, hold the horses when the Progress arrives, flog tickets, ice-creams at the interval and do some prompting. If you're Shakespeare, it's a breeze.'

'I am Shakespeare still', replied William.

There were several reasons for the astonishing rise of Drama in the late sixteenth century. Of these, the main one was the collapse of everything else. The Reformation had seen to it that no-one went to Church any more. It was too easy to get blown up by a Catholic, pointed at by a Puritan or anaesthetised by an Anglican.

Those who could read Prose, quite sensibly didn't as the choice was between someone nicknamed Lyly and a person called Nashe. Prose and the Church, faced with dwindling appeal in a short-term Renaissance market, combined reluctantly to do the only thing they could – release a safe Bible. However, the public, painfully unfamiliar with this concept and more than a little anxious not to be chopped, stretched or roasted again,

wouldn't touch it. Poetic Drama stepped from the wings as Literature's other tills, with a whimper, went to.

Chapman looked incredulously at his pay-slip. 'What's income tax, Philip?'

'The old days were really the worst,' said Henslowe, flying into a tangent sweeping his books sideways into the ear of a fallen head – making Burbage hiccup portentously. Ben shot a startled glance sideways; and then downwards, with gathering dislike. Not only had the great actor been quaffing his precious *aurum potabile*, thereby ruining the experiment, but he had missed his magniloquent peroration on how to construct Works.

'Extra!' roared Ben.

'Outside' translated Chapman meekly, as the unprotesting Burbage was bundled to the door – along with an antique hat stand that had not answered to Ben's satisfaction on Roman Tragedy.

Beaumont and Fletcher tore a page in half, offered each other another drink and wandered out to have a look.

'It was a battle in the old days' continued Henslowe, more at his ease. 'Imagine tramping the provinces looking for a town when the authorities didn't want you. They kept turning the signs round. We'd get back to the same bunch of yokels we'd just left and they'd nick the money back. Three times into Accrington and I was ready to give up. Now with the Theatres we get the money on the way in. And the authorities are chuffed because all the trouble's in one place: anyone who's had a few canaries and just looking to get into a play, can go outside the city walls for it.

Things got going a bit, I suppose, with the Wets as Ben used to call them. University boys, camp as a row of tents, not his mug of beer at all. Of course they all hated the Church and the City, but they still wanted to do something commercial, something dressy. But what with the state of the trade in those days some of the weaker ones got very upset. You'd have to see to believe what we had coming in here as actors. The only chap with the answer – I've got him in my wallet here somewhere – was young Kitty Marlowe. 'Look Pip', he said, 'Just give me one good pair of lungs and I'll do you a play'.

Well, I remember the first afternoon of Tamburlaine. We just couldn't get them all in. It was worse than Drake getting back at Tilbury. Anyhow old Kitty reckoned the play was a tragedy – till I raced round at half-time that is and told him. 'They like it! Don't kill him!!' So, cool as a quick thousand, he just flipped out my pen, turned a funeral into a wedding, and back they all came next week. And he still made sure we were washing that stage four hours later – wedding or no wedding. He was an artist all right. Mind you, he nearly walked out on us once. Faustus was leafing through this book, wondering where Helen of Troy had got to, and we were doing our nuts trying to find little Robin Peach, so I collared this groundling urchin and shoved him out there. Faustus couldn't believe it.

Was THIS the face that launched a thousand ships?

But you see they didn't mind in the audience. Anything about travel, they loved it. And the further away the better, so Kitty was always down with the sailors finding out where everyone had been. The page was his globe all right – Africa, Mongolia, Babylon, Bithynia – left us standing for props. Didn't know where to look for what most of the time. Didn't matter though. Stuck a tiger in Carthage once, and they wanted him in every scene. I tell you we had an encore for elephants in Paris. Still all those days ended when Walsingham's boys thought Kitty was asking too many questions down at the docks. 'The playwright who knew too much' they said. One night he never came back, which was not unusual so we waited till the next night, and still no Kitty. He'd been done for – and by that lot down at the Rose Theatre. I didn't think they'd go on playing to a couple of tinkers and a dog for ever. So then we had to let them have it good and proper. Hired a bloke with the plague to go and mingle – and the whole place had to be burnt down. Anyhow, got a new play for me then have you Chappers?'

'Yes,' said Chapman philosophically.

'Everyman has a book on Shakespeare in him' is a well-known academic proverb. It is no secret that the Industry is now capable of filling Warwickshire four times over. So let us enjoy some all-too-brief moments of common sense.

The accuracy of the Shakespearean texts need not worry a normal, healthy student. Generally, it is a study best reserved for those who read all of 'Paradise Lost' without being told to. Regarding the chronology of the plays this – both from correlation with the precise facts of history and over-whelming internal evidence – is clearly alphabetical. My only canonical reservation would be the accepted lumping of 'King Lear' with the Quieter Bedroom Farces. The Henslowe Edition of Shakespeare is the most expensive and comes with a free cup and ball. The Wisconsin Edition on the other hand is mainly useful for my introduction: "Shakespeare bestrode the moon, where others couldn't even find Calais" being a particularly handy, all-purpose tribute.

At a time when Shakespearean criticism can tell one as much about the play as Mrs Lincoln, it is a relief to fondle J. Trafalgar Wilson's 'Pericles, Bottom and The

Fool'. Most of the book is taken up with the great 'Unsex me here' debate, which has always been a problem for intepreters of 'Macbeth'. Trafalgar Wilson sorts out where, in terms of biology and Scottish castle architecture, this delicate operation might have taken place, before wondering why a fourteen-year-old posing as a Scottish Queen should want to say this, when the warning note in 'The Merchant of Venice' is quite clear.

> There's a divinity that shapes our ends
> Rough-hew them how we will.

He is good on adolescent pressures in Denmark, and most persuasive on diet and trustworthiness in 'Julius Caesar', making a well-argued case for a fly-weight Brutus. He looks at the social setting of the Elizabethan Theatre and has severe doubts whether cock-fighting and bear-baiting were ever going to go anywhere. Indeed, he says, 'The continuing regard for Shakespeare's plays leaves us no finer testament to the transience of bear-baiting'. Wilson's book can serve to show us all that, in Shakespearean scholarship, there is still room at the top – unlike the rest of Elizabethan Drama where one usually ends up taking T. S. Eliot's word for it and two supporting quotations.

'So it's within a hundred miles of Venice then?' flashed Henslowe, subsiding nonchalantly into his Diary: 'At ve Door. Murano-Glaff Pigeons, Flides, Poftcards. Plafter Machiavelf in ve ftyle ov Onyx.'

'And what sort of play is it, Will?'

'I don't know. I think it's one of my Problem Plays.'

'We can't sell that!'

'All right, it's a tragi-pastorical revenge comedy then.'

'That's better' purred Henslowe, 'we can use that. Very intriguing. That'll get them gawking at the posters. Tragi-pastorical revenge comedy. Quite a student of human nature aren't you, Will?'

'Life is my work. Everybody is my contemporary.'

'Sorry, Will, what was that?'

'I am everybody's contemporary.'

'Yes. Good. Fine. Well, that's all right then. Now, Will, let's hear some of this play. Full of quotes is it?'

While Henslowe lit a cigar Chapman leaned philosophically over William's shoulder. Beaumont and Fletcher surreptitiously fed their twin sharpener and moved closer. Even Ben and Burbage fell silent except for the occasional oath.

Twelth ado about something or other (Part one)

Dramatis personae

CURIO: *leaning son of the Duke of Pisa*

CURIO'S FOOL

EMILIA

BIANCA: *daughters of the Duke*

ANGELO

BALTHAZAR: *servant to Curio*

DON ARMADILLO: *Spanish suitor to Emilia*

VITTORIO: *in love with Emilia*

LORENZO: *in exile*

ENGLISH LORDS: *waging war in Italy*

MISTRESS MERRYTITS: *a bawd*

CLOTHEARS: *a clown*

GHOST

MESSENGERS: *passim*

TORRES: *Armadillo's servant*

The Court is in mourning for the Duke, shipwrecked off the coast of Milan, when he returns, although it is really Angelo in disguise. Hearing of what has passed, Don Armadillo, intending to seduce Emilia, runs Vittorio through having gone into the wrong bedroom, the effect of a potion poured on his moustache by Torres his servant. By way of amendment, Curio kills a messenger. Meanwhile, Merrytits and Clothears have come across the dejected Lorenzo. The plot is successful, until Balthazar arrives, also disguised as the Duke. Curio, his suspicions confirmed at last, kills Torres. At once, Don Armadillo demands satisfaction and tries to seduce Merrytits. News is brought that the English army is outside the city walls, so Curio, fearing for his safety, sends out his Fool to do battle. The Fool entertains the

67

marauders so well, that Angelo is tricked into revealing his true identity. At last, Lorenzo returns and kills Balthazar, whom he imagines has been guarding his chastity from Emilia. Curio, enraged, strangles a ghost but is allowed to go free. At the end Angelo repents and decides to become the Duke again, offering his hand to the overjoyed Merrytits. Clothears pacifies the invaders, now led by the Fool, and there is a grand wedding reception where Emilia is sent to the English troops as a present. She confesses to being Bianca all along, which sends Don Armadillo mad, and Lorenzo into a passionate declaration of love. Merrytits calls for a double marriage and the English troops join in with much carousing.

Meanwhile Merrytits and Clothears have come across the dejected Lorenzo.

Act two, *Scene three*

Enter MERRYTITS *and* CLOTHEARS

M: What ho, Linen Lugs! Here we are up the creek of Arden.

C: O woe, woe, misery, woe and more woe.

M: Tush, I'll give no more ear to thy thread. But tis prettily watered clown.

C: I'll speak it a green spinney an you knit me a balaclava, Blithe Bobbers.

M: Tis all one. Faith, here's a Merry Andrew.

Enter LORENZO *with hoop and stick.*
Exit hoop, alone.
Exit LORENZO *in pursuit with stick.*
Re-enter hoop, unbothered.
Re-enter LORENZO, *hurling stick at disappearing hoop.*

M: Methinks thou wilt stick at nothing coz.

C: Marry, tis a glutinous remark.

L: Art thou easily cock-a-hoop sweet maid? Prithee, thy name.

68

M: Merrytits, an't please your lordship.
C: Aye, tis a merry chest.
L: Soft.
M: Spungey perchance.
C: But tis all meet.
L: Then call me Lory and have truck.
M: Pray sir, I have no licence.
L: Twere better to have no licence, that shows
   thee truckleplated.
C: Troth, what a pair!

Exeunt.

Clothears pacifies the invaders, now led by the Fool.

Act five, *Scene four*

*Before the walls of Pisa. The English Camp. Trumpets.
Alarum. Flourish. Enter* THE FOOL *with* BATTERSEA,
RUTLAND, CHALFONT ST GILES, CROYDON UPPINGHAM
and HULL

C St. G: My liege, tis full seven times that Phoebus
         Hath drawn o'er the chariots of morning –
         To light our men's slavering at the ramparts,
         Bedecked with a white flag unfurled –
         God grant we may soon thrash the Pisan
         puppy.
     U: Wherein Pisan mothers have cause to quake.
     F: Why is a frog like unto an elephant, Hull?
     H: I know not, my liege.
     F: Well, do any of you? (*Silence*) All right. What
        makes a fishmonger greedy?
     R: My liege, thy wise drift hath beaten us all.

Enter CLOTHEARS. *The Lords fall to their swords.*

     C: Perchance tis his business makes him sell fish?
     F: Excellent.
     B: Ever the breath of Mars swells our banners

And glaring-eyed madness is all around.

F: Can February March?

C: Nay, but April May.

Enter a Messenger, in haste.

M: My pants betray the urgency I speak. . . .

U: Out, scurvy wretch!

R: Revolting cur!

They fall upon him. CLOTHEARS and THE FOOL walk aside, arm in arm.

F: The best way to keep a woman's love?

C: Why, coz, tis not to return it.

F: I' faith, now is the summer of my amusement
   – No more unto the breach dear friends.

Exeunt, stepping over the Messenger.

While Drama is at its height, it would be intellectually slap-dash to ignore the concepts of Tragedy and Comedy. However, a willingness on the part of my colleagues to overlook the obvious has always bedevilled this type of discussion. Comedy, to be exact, is a series of practical jokes ending in marriage. Tragedy, on the other hand, is not quite so gloomy, ending, generally, in death. Although an American scholar has found that tragic heroes tend to be heavier smokers, I would, none the less, prefer to recommend 'The Uniquet Unicorn: Readings in the Structure of Judaeo-Christian Tragedy' by Reverend Septimus Tibbs (an elderly theologian in a dark suit, always ready with a peppermint) and Dr Wassily Cossack (fond of discussing a subjective view of Tragedy over 100% grain spirit and salt cucumbers). After three hundred and fifty pages, they both conclude that the only acceptable definition of Tragedy is 'birth'.

Similarly, the distinction between Elizabethan and Jacobean Drama is not a difficult matter, provided easily excitable people suffering with withdrawal symptoms from the Renaissance are not allowed to get away with alarmist phrases like 'Spirit of the Age' etc. Jacobean Drama is simply a term of abuse applied to any play between Guy Fawkes Night and 1625, which is both utterly improbable and extraordinarily nasty. Particularly ludicrous bits are known as 'conventions'. So, in essence, Jacobean Drama was Elizabethan Drama that got worse. It was because the groundlings and dramatists imagined villainy to be as natural to Italy as the average accountant imagines sex to be compulsory in Sweden, that we have been left with a whole mortuary of such Boris Karloff plays as 'A New Way To Bury Old Bodies' and 'Tis a Pity She's A Skull'.

Act one, *Scene them all*

(Enter the Cardinal's servant, Stiletto, munching a bat and dragging a skeleton full of maggots)

> S: She will ne'er recognise her lordship's bones
> For long have vultures spewed his poisonous flesh
> O'er us all –
> But yet, tis not her widow's weeds –
> That cling –
> And darken her shape to this verminous world,
> Tis lust for her brother that wracks her body
> In unnatural torment. –

(Enter the Duke's widow screaming round in circles)

DW: Oh! Oh! AaaaaaaH! Mmmmmm! Ugh!
Aaaaaaaaaaaaaaaaaaah!

S: Alas, such infectious fraternity
Carries a grave penalty i' the end.

(Stiletto lovingly unsheathes a long, blunt, rusty knife – a saw, an axe, a hammer, a length of cheese wire, a pair of rubber boots, bucket and road-drill)

S: How fares your ladyships this black night
When only whores and screech owls go forth?

DW: Stiletto my friend I am sore disquiet.
Yet I see thou hast physic for me
To lighten the burden of my flat soul.

S: How closely she fishes!

(Stiletto wraps a cheese wire round her neck)

DW: Ah, thy hands token endless relief,
Though tis a little tight, Stiletto.

S: A thousand pardons, your ladyship.

DW: UUUUURRRRRRRRRGH!

(Exit Stiletto. She dies and hits the floor. The head falls from the Duke's skeleton and rolls towards her, spilling teeth)

Head: Life shtill breefsh in me shlowly my Dushesh.

DW: And I my Duke am not yet gone this world –
Wilt thou make me immortal with a kiss?

Head: One kish and I'll shlip away.
DW: Oh, I die.

(They die. Re-enter Stiletto with portable gallows, slips up, hangs himself)

S: Now I see from my height this cursed orb
Is a cesspool wherein we all betimes must drown.

(He dies)

Drama like this appealed to such increasingly bizarre instincts that not only did the groundlings begin to smell atrocious – but the Puritans came out in all weathers to suggest loudly the combustible nature of everyone present. Drama duly retreated behind closed doors, for evening performances to which only wealthy and consenting adults were invited. The seeds of the Civil War were sown.

The groundlings weren't too bothered, but the Puritans were very upset, insisting that weird Drama like this actually did give Pleasure, and should therefore be stamped out at once. In fact, all Drama should be stopped. Hadn't it, they shrieked, all been the same money-spinning thing about foreigners hoaxing, swindling and murdering one another?

The King, clearly disturbed that 'The Mayflower' didn't have enough room for all these loons, immediately ordered the construction of bigger ships. The Puritans countered by demanding the conversion of theatres into churches – or warehouses for dried raisins. The King replied that Drama had a Divine Right to exist, and called upon supporters of the idea to buy spaniels, wear flamboyant clothes and look confident. The Puritans ordered their squad to find boring clothes, look crackers and prepare for war. That the result was a full-scale Civil War only goes to show that enough people were taking notice of Religion once again.

Chapter Six

Drama and Religion paid the price of their folly in the next century when no-one took any notice of them. But for the meantime we must return to the seventeenth century, and the spectacle of the entire nation busily shoving pykes into each other. Now, there is nothing wrong with shoving a pyke into someone, if it's what you want to do, and provided no-one gets hurt, but pruning the King is something else. It carries with it a serious penalty – in this case Charles II – and a restoration of just the type of Drama to make the Puritans look right after all. Alas, theatres were brothels, Mrs Worthington's first daughters did not – in all faith – tend to hang about, and the average playgoer expected to consult more than the programme in this nice little place out of the rain. Drama has a lot to answer for before we even consider its worst effect which was, undoubtedly, on Poetry and Prose. Impoverished, and fully aware that they couldn't put up a decent Civil War if the Puritans got difficult, Poetry and Prose turned practical, in an effort to appear indispensible. Science, Religion and Politics now filled their pages.

Women, of course, had to accept a few changes in this world of serious, masculine endeavour.

Poetry certainly went a bit strange on them. John Donne had got together with some of his more metaphysical friends and worked out Poemetry. This was an argumentative way of measuring one's passions with the latest scientific instruments. Poemetry, for all its logos, didn't need to scan and could pretty much rhyme when it felt like it. As a sort of warm-up to this brain-cracking stuff, the poets all agreed to adopt names which no one had a hope of pronouncing correctly. Donne started things off by wishing to be known as Donny, Herbert thought he gained something from being articulated as Hair-Butt, while the Carew Estate have spent centuries down at the London Sorting Office looking for old letters about Poemetry addressed to a 'Mr. Curry'.

Later on when Poemetry rose above ladies, to square up with God, the angle of composition remained congruent: the first line was still the best one. Compare Donne's beautiful 'Sonnet To A Socket Set', beginning with the uncanny:

'Clear off all you other Tools –'

– where his mistress is, in turn, all the parts that go to make up a really tight job – with Herbert's moving exhortation at the outset of 'The Steps':

'Christ hold the ladder –'

It would be tempting at this point to quote Crashaw's 'The Sky Wrench', were one to forget John Donne's provocative, pioneering poem, 'The Reckoning':

> Lousy old hour-glass, unruly compass,
>> Twice or thrice have I measur'd with thee
>> Eclipsing the center of Love's Destiny
>>> And would have thrown thee in the sea –
> But now the centrique part in tears of hope
>> I chart, not thou, with Love's New Deciders
>> Mandrake root, protractor, goe Dividers
>>> Twixt parallel fingers,
> And say only thy love, not mine, can telescope
>> So I may carry it compact to Afrique
>> Yet know, to thee, long since forsook
>>> That I, very probably, colossal look –
> Till gray haires, yes, concentrique
>> Do protract my return to thee,

Thine eye bent, unbending me by Degree
Mathematic and by now arthritic
Ruled and still as logs are we
   Look do you want any more of mee?

Quite clearly, for ladies, the good old days were over. Once, the arrival of a poem had made them giggle, flush and hear bird-song, race the footman through a minuet and throw cushions at the maid, order six new petticoats, and then retire to the sofa, to hug piles of laundry, and dream of long journeys to strange lands. But now when a poem arrived, ladies just went pale, felt confused and vaguely threatened for a while, and then slid the thing in among bills. They didn't like being analysed.

But then they weren't to know that Milton was on the way, and that soon they would be scrambling in among pyramids of bills wistfully eager to re-read those unusual, sweet little boffin bards with their lovely ideas about altimeters, pendulums, plumb-lines . . . or anything.

'Shit creek, thy name is woman' is the confident summary of Milton's work I remember from an Australian colleague, particularly as it was fired repeatedly and loudly at the Emeritus Professor of Engineering, in one of those apocalyptic moments which invariably follow a crate of the College's eighty-five year old brandy. It is an interesting point from which to begin.

John Milton blamed many things on women – in fact, everything. The fair sex were, at the very least, a theological mistake, biological after-thought and economic encumbrance. But then he was a bit like that. He tended to think on a grand scale. His eloquent call for the legalisation of divorce upon grounds of incompatibility was, to him, only the first vital step in negotiating a separate planet for women. And their daughters. Indeed his love-letters, with the habitually soft opening 'Dear Spare Rib', are a treasure house of warnings and counter-threats in which he frequently indicated a realm of the universe where women might like to congregate.

Among his contemporaries, there was no doubt that the Fall of Man would eventually be his subject. Everybody had done Arthur; and Alfred wouldn't be any good, with its crude suggestion that post-lapsarian man can't look after himself in a kitchen. So that left Adam. But a long way off yet.

For seven years in the wilderness, Milton got ready. He lay awake at nights in a lonely, rented Buckingham-shire cottage wondering whether to write in Urdu or Rumanian, till a friend asked him what was wrong with English? Deeply impressed by this question, Milton adopted the friend as his coach, and developed astonishing powers. 'You don't like the meal. You hate it. Thirteen lines. Fifty seconds. Go –' shot the coach, and Milton's reply soared back:

> Now with darkness descending, Hunger appeared:
> Darts dreadful of force incredible sped
> Through stomach long-waiting for carnal repast;
> Then down along stairs to the kitchen I dropped
> As if to Canaan nuptials repairing,
> To find a room, magnificent with steam
> And promise meaty at the table set;
> Yet O woman! What can this offal mean?
> No longer with gaze nor sapient forkful
> Could man this Thyestean rubbish consume!
> Stew yclep'd, with all God's Grace beholden,
> Yet would Christ himself seek recompense for this
> Till sinuous Tigris in Euphrates falls.

His technique got stronger. His knowledge lapped Chaucer's. But his adrenalin was going down. Again, his old friend, with whom he'd re-written the school syllabus at the age of three, had the answer. Two hours a day down at Horton Horticultural Hall, full of the sort of women who annoyed him, and then straight back home for a row with the wife. His spirits picked up. The time was getting very close for him to be famous.

It was now that Milton formed the intention of entering the International Epic Contest, under the auspices of two buried Greeks. Announcing his subject to a hushed Western World, apart from silly, whittering noises which greeted his scheme 'to horrify God with the ways of women', he invited a team of astronomers, linguists, Rabbis, librarians, flautists, physiotherapists and, of course, divorce lawyers to join him for the finishing mental touches to his long preparation.

In 1658, the team was sent away. He was ready. Now he was on his own. One Tuesday afternoon it suddenly started:

> 'Of Man's first disobedience, and the fruit
> Of that forbidden tree, whose mortal taste . . .'

Unfortunately, the first volume of 'Paradise Lost' was indeed lost as both daughters were out, and the milkman couldn't get very far with it all. Yet his daughters did manage to get the rest of it down, despite the butcher and the gardener getting the odd, unwelcome earful, and flogged it for £10. Encouraged by ten quid for the bad news, Milton had every hope of retirement after 'Paradise Regained'. Readers took a more cautious view: if defeat took up 12 Volumes, what was a victory going to be worth?

At this stage I suppose it is timely to answer the question every scholar hates. No, I haven't read it – but then neither has Sam Johnson, and he wrote a dictionary. I expect, if the truth is known, most people take the easy way in at Volume 9. Anyhow, Milton never had to read 'Paradise Lost'.

Milton Prepares

Ladies were beginning to get rather fed up with the seventeenth century. In fact, they were on the verge of going out with painters when, suddenly, poems started arriving from people with names like Lovelace, Suckling, Sir Charles Sedley, the Earl of Rochester. They weren't Puritans; and they didn't sound metaphysical. Could it be true at last? Were romantic Cavaliers going to sweep them up onto white chargers at midnight with the electrifying whisper of a foreign destination? Well, no. What was more likely was the arrival of an erratic coach at any hour of the night which would pull up noisily and then appear to have no occupant, until bewigged rumblings from the floor of the carriage indicated life, or rather suspended animation, in the shape of a sloshed gentleman solicitous of a temporary and vigorous loan of the lady's private parts.

This sexual ambassador would normally be carrying two claret-splashed poems with him. One about frigidity should the poor dear say 'no'. And one about whores should the little cracker say 'yes' far too quickly. What the gentleman expected was hopeless surrender – fair enough – but after some small, token resistance at least. Ladies began to realise that their most important asset was, quite simply, how they did it. That they had to do it somehow was not in question, since they had now become crumpet: recreational ego-boosting items of most use between wars and after work. Or maybe all day if there was nothing else to do. Such was their demise, and it seemed complete. But it wasn't. At large in London was the man with the final insult.

John Dryden just ignored them completely. Didn't even mention them. Although there was one occasion when he alluded to his wife, on her tombstone:

> Here lies my wife, here let her lie,
> Now she's at rest – and so am I.

I suppose this is the reason why, even today, ladies tend to go a bit quiet if the word Dryden crops up. But it is possible that he didn't write this elegy after all. To start with, he was never actually at rest. Shiploads of a new brown bean coming up the Thames had seen to that.

Things happened to Dryden that had never happened to anyone before. In the grips of the new brown bean, he came to rely upon a dark, morning mugful to weld his senses to each new day. Fuelled by the pod, the days rushed by. His eyes widened, his pulse rocketed, his wig lifted. A strange conviction overtook him that the eighteenth century had already started. Haunted by dreams of bubbling percolators, his body twitching to their intimate gurgle, his mind gradually went epigrammatic.

On March 15th, 1666 on Saturday at midday Dryden began to speak in rhyming couplets – experiencing at the same time, a terrific urge to attack everybody in sight. This could have led to embarrassing complications – such as an eventual lack of targets – if Dryden hadn't patented an amusing system involving a handkerchief, a pin, and the disagreeable end of a donkey to decide his political and religious outlooks for each month. Yet, even with most of inner London chiselled into little verbal coffins, Dryden still felt somehow restless. Wasn't there someone else he could have a go at? He took to long walks with his thermos flask. One day, grappling with the beaker in a quiet country churchyard the answer came to him: if he invented Literary Criticism he could unearth a whole, posthumous world – full of targets. This, on a tide of caffeine, Dryden did – but far beyond the calls of mere writer-bashing. He started re-writing it for them.

Dryden's surplus energy was a legend in his own life-time. He was an incredible man, a media-man-of-the-moment-man, revamping, mixing, combining, cutting, pasting, not even Shakespeare was safe. He pops up everywhere: re-doing 'Hamlet' as a musical, sung in the original Danish; in a postscript to the only art exhibition Molière ever gave; with a play on Restoration Night, a bit of routine, commission work 'Charles, King of England'; in a satirical essay on tea; auditioning someone to dance the pillars in his pantomime 'Samson Agonistes'; persuading an interview out of a Puritan dissident, before writing a long poem in the form of a Socratic dialogue about wringing short stories out of Chaucer's Ballads etc. etc. But his best subject, the one he never tired of, perhaps the quintessential theme of all his writing, the area where he felt most truly at home, was Shadwell – and vice versa. Pepys was there:

'Met Mr Dryden. Says Shadwell has the pox.'
'Met Mr Shadwell. Says Dryden's wife should know.'
'Met Mr Dryden. Shatwell, begotten in buggery, has more diseases than a French hospital. With brass knobs on.'
'Met Mr Shadwell. Dryden a filthy, cankered, parboiled rat. And no returns.'
'Met Mr Dryden. Shatsmell a stinking, swaggering turd.'
'Met Mr Shadwell. Dryden never of human parentage. And a fucking bastard. Smells of rotten cabbage.'
'Met Mr Dryden. The cunt. If I get hold of him, I'll ram his fucking wig . . .'

While Messrs. Dryden and Shadwell were taking up military positions, the rest of the country had other things to do. The Merry Monarch was back. And, oh, what a time it was! Knickers flew from Parliament, empty flagons rolled through the streets. Pepys didn't get home for a week, young actresses found themselves drinking enormous amounts of episcopal sherry and everywhere the joyous song arose, from scented chaises-longues, underneath hedges and on top of makeshift tables:

> Let the Nation's organs swell
> And ev'ry Charlie 'ave 'is Nell!
> Wrap 'er in a cloak,
> Shove 'er up an oak,
> And dance three times round Boscobel!

Drama had the time of its life with its new Master of the Revels. The King took a personal interest in it – not just to the extent of seeing that the leading actresses got home all right and leaving his carriage outside all night just to make sure everything was all right, and could he just ring the Palace? etc. but also as Royal Adviser on textual matters. It was a necessary office – seeing as most of the libertine Dramatists had the shakes, and no teeth at 23. Whenever they were a bit careless, leaving a character without his oats, or the leading lady with no chance to flash her legs, then Charles would lean into the manuscript with a honeyed pen and put the thing right.

The Plain Way To a Wife of Mode

by Wychgreverege

Dramatis personae

DORIBEL, *a rakish fop, in love with Melinda.*

PHILLIMENT, *brother to Melinda, suitor to Rosabel, a man of fashion and a rake.*

MR PINK, *eternal suitor to Mrs Hardlook, a beau, and a rake.*

SIR DITHERING FORTUNE, *a fine gentleman and rake, in love with Rosabel and Melinda.*

LORD LIMP, *an old rake.*

JUBILEE, *a young spade, and servant to Lord Limp.*

BETTY, *woman to Melinda, highly prized by Lord Limp.*

ROSABEL, *niece to Lord Limp, in love with Doribel.*

MELINDA, *sister to Philliment, in love with Mr Pink, but more than a bit interested in Jubilee.*

MRS TINSELTRAP, *a fading gossip, and lady of quality, in love secretly with Philliment.*

MRS HARDLOOK, *a young lady of fashion, hoping to corner Sir Dithering Fortune.*

MRS CABBAGE, *pretty young widow of an old country squire.*

Footmen, Chairmen, Men of the Watch, a Clergyman.

Mrs Tinseltrap, cherishing a secret passion for Philliment, arranges with Men of the Watch for him to discover a love-letter, in which Rosabel apparently accepts Sir Dithering. Philliment, stricken, rushes out to report that Melinda was seen leaving Sir Dithering's lodgings early one morning with a cup of sugar. This doesn't seem to impress Doribel who carries on sleeping with Betty. However, Mrs Hardlook (*Breeches for this one, please. Charles.*) is interested, and agrees to support the story if Philliment will impersonate a titled uncle to charm Sir Dithering. Mrs Tinseltrap hears of the story, and gleefully adds Rosabel to it, with shoes in hand. Sir Dithering, meanwhile, decides to admit that such events might have happened, in a loose attempt to discourage Doribel and Philliment from their suit of Melinda and Rosabel, hoping, at worst, to have one of them if his plan is only half-successful.

(*Try and get him in bed with both of them, then do what you like. Perhaps Jubilee could come in with a feather duster, see them there, and just sort of join in. Charles.*)

Mrs Hardlook is horrified at this; and plans revenge on Philliment by persuading Mrs Cabbage that a cushion under the dress is the latest fashion at tea-time, as is holding a snuff-box, in this case Philliment's, and promptly invites Mrs Tinseltrap over for tea. The spectacle of a pregnant Mrs Cabbage fondling Philliment's snuff-box causes Mrs Tinseltrap to spend the next week in bed, where the ever-casual Doribel occasionally joins her. (*Yes. That's a good idea. Charles.*)

Seeing his chance at last Mr Pink calls upon Mrs Hardlook with a concocted proof of Sir Dithering's philandering, along with Philliment posing as his wealthy grandfather, whereby Mrs Hardlook is deceived into accepting his proposal. In return for this favour, Mr Pink snubs Melinda (*After a pretty randy farewell scene I hope. Good tits on Melinda, please. Charles.*) despite Betty's appearance as Melinda's aunt with the title deeds to a country house as a birthday present, which enables Philliment to seek repayment from Doribel in the form of a pretended match with Mrs Cabbage to cure Rosabel of her love for him.

In the meantime Lord Limp (*Recognisably, a thin caricature of the Lord Privy Seal Rothmere OK? Old bore walked right in on me twice last week. I'll see you're all right. Charles.*), thinking he is turning the screws on Betty by threatening to go and fight the Dutch, only succeeds in firing Mrs Cabbage with passion. A clergyman is brought at once, and, secretly, they are wed.

Now believing Doribel is lost to Mrs Cabbage, Rosabel consents to Philliment's proposal, while Doribel wins Melinda, still weak from Mr Pink's rejection of her advances. However, Mrs Tinseltrap is getting better, and eager to get one back at Mrs Hardlook, spreads the word that Mr Pink is bankrupt. Sir Dithering, his plan in ruins, is no longer in any fit condition to resist Mrs Hardlook's renewed onslaught, and the match is contracted. (*Hmm! That one I want to see. No-one else on stage. Minimum of props. Charles.*) Mrs Tinseltrap then visits Mr Pink, having heard of his wealthy grandfather; while Mr Pink has learnt from Mrs Hardlook that Mrs Tinseltrap is a lady of very generous circumstances. They soon yield to each others' advances – made with crushing flattery – and straightaway the marriage is made. (*Make sure Mrs T. plays up 'the older woman' bit here. Plenty of winks and brazen remarks. Maybe some thigh. Charles.*) Alas, the truth comes out when the first bill comes in, and the play ends with both lambasting each other for being false, and wondering whether the fare to London was worth it.

The play, in due course, went on down at The King's Theatre, and ran successfully for nine weeks in a row. Although for the amount of notice anyone took of it, it might as well have run for the next nine years. Samuel Pepys reviews the play in his Diary. He was fond of the theatre. He normally got there about mid-afternoon, after a good morning's work and a barrel of oysters at lunchtime:

Up, and to my office all the morning, whither by and by comes Mrs Evelyn. She, as usual, would fain have my Diary for her husband's use, but I, looking splendid in a new black cloth suit lined with silk Francais, had her: deux fois sur le desk et cinque fois sur le mantelpiece. Thence at noon to the Dog and Duck for lunch, where Susan the pot-maid did let me throw her breasts in the air, I being mightily pleased and merry all the time. So to Mr Tinkle's where I did buy a metal Triangle. Cost me 5s. Thence to the King's Playhouse at 3 o'clock to see a new comedy, The Plain Way To a Wife of Mode by Mr Wychgreverege. This prettily acted, though Mrs Fastgirdle's legs, being the talk of all the town, did trouble me mightily whereby mine own were not easy in the crossing. However that wrought well with me, for I did spy Partridge's wife and made her sit with me and listen to my triangle, while I, having opportunity, did dally with hers and towzle her breasts et j'étais très vite sur le job en criant Geronimo et je l'ai rogeré vingt fois avant Act II. Après les ice-creams, and she being gone, moi refreshed did a little tour of the boxes ou j'ai trouvé Bangwell's wife se penchant over the balcony en regardant le play. Tout de suite j'ai fait sortir mon collègue en pensant hey ho, hey ho, c'est au travail nous allons; et j'étais bien en derrière quattorze fois. Lorsque le play était nearly finished so aussi was mon collègue et j'ai went home in a chair. Cost me 2s., but needed same. And so to supper, prayers and Bed.

The nation couldn't go on like this – however upset Charles was about the Puritans. It was all right, for a while, to do Royalist things like random sex, twenty-four hour drinking and marrying late, if still alive, but somewhere along the line the country had to pull itself together. A few shocks helped. First of all, the pox wiped out most of London in 1665. Then some libertine, attempting a late-night pipe, set the whole city on fire. Then Parliament realised there was no money left because – basically – Charles had spent it; and mainly on non-retrievable toilet luxuries. Just for after-shave and crested mink loo rolls you were talking about six hundred grand. The country, now looking rather pale, began to see the need for a change. Eventually, even the King's most loyal courtiers were under some kind of strain to show any interest in hearing about his Divine Nights.

When the Merry Monarch died, not surprisingly of natural causes, people welcomed William and Mary, a couple going steady, domestic, sturdy, pious etc. and Decency returned. No-one went to the theatre. No-one felt like writing plays. Everyone was so ashamed. The lights went out all over England again, at a respectable hour, and things actually got done before noon. The nation's moral holiday was over.

With Drama effectively out of action, and destined to stay that way for 200 years, its old enemy Prose reared its printed head, although in the seventeenth century it hadn't been up to much. I suppose it had, with one appalling exception, attracted quite a good sort of person though. There was Sir Thomas Browne who had tried to write the world's longest sentence while Sir Francis Bacon – in his lighter moments – was composing quotations. Izaak Walton chipped in with a book to say that anglers were special people, while Sir Robert Burton listed things that depressed him and sort of what it felt like. Then there was John Bunyon. He wrote a mysteriously popular book called 'A Pilgrim's Progess' which contains the literary understatement of all time: 'I have used similitudes'. He was unfortunately, a tinker who kept saying that the world was going to end, and singled out various dates for this event. As each passed without incident, people were moved to ask him what he was on about. The reply was a simple one: the world had ended but nobody had noticed. He, of course, spent most of his life locked up.

So it is there for everyone to see. Prose, over eight hundred years old, was still not in good shape. Another duff century after this one, and it would have been lucky to have been used in letters. But something happened at the eleventh hour to rouse literary gentlemen into getting it going. The Royal Society of Scientists – full of new things to say now that an apple had hit Newton on the head, Galileo had cleaned his telescope, and Harvey had realised that blood didn't sink down to your boots when you got up – had produced a report to say that Prose was incompetent for their uses. There is no lower breed of insult to a literary man, and the next hundred years was Prose all the way.

end galley

The Augustan Dream

The eighteenth century got off to a roaring start. It was going to be man's best century so far, it said. It was going to be an Age of Reason. Instances of vulgarity, ignorance and filth were to be dismissed as 'very seventeenth century'. It was going to see a time when people were rational, polite, knowledgeable, decorous and tasteful. This, in short, was the Augustan Dream.

Now, to see this Age of Reason in an academic perspective, I think one has to realise that every century likes to feel that its inhabitants are, on the whole, having a pretty reasonable time, and that once one has grasped this, one has to move on and ask how the eighteenth century proposed to make its own time especially reasonable? And then I think one finds the answer straightaway.

In the meantime what are we to make of the Men of Letters? Were they in any way sheepish about the civilising task which lay ahead of them? They certainly look a bit sheepish. Darwin might well have had second thoughts looking at some of them. In fact, perpetually bleating out 'Sir', socially herding round clubs to do this in strict pecking order at dinner time whilst medically experiencing gout, pox, dropsicals and barnacles all the time there would seem to be an overwhelming element of Ba-ba Podgicus about them.

Anyhow, were these men going to be able to do it? At times they must have wondered whether Reason itself hadn't gone on a Grand Tour.

Two Oxford and Charterhouse men moved in on this dreadful situation at once. Sir Richard Steele undertook to sort out a few basic things in a series of articles for the 'Tatler' about not flinging week-old bed-pans over pedestrians, not letting some quack cut off your wrist for hayfever, and not otter-baiting, quail-bashing and rat-fighting when they could be playing cricket – even if they were going to make it look like croquet with hockey sticks – while Mr Joseph Addison made himself available for the profferment of more refined advice through the pages of the 'Spectator'. He would indicate how, for example, to smile; to eat breakfast; to walk; to sit down on leather chairs; even how to die with aplomb. The whole thing was not unlike certain magazines for young women of the what-you-must-know-about-Mozart-for-dinner-parties type. And, like these, Mr Addison answered letters. A lady from the country writes:

Dear Jozuff,

Oik ort at liddle brat o' moin skoffin' bred agin. Taint furze toim as ow's 'appened, an oi tole 'im 'at 'is air'll fall owt if ee's a moind to do it more. Well, larst toim, oi 'ad er clozer luk at wot eed bin a-doin ov, an oim wurrid. Wuzz more 'an juss bred. 'Ad jam an budder on ut. An eed gon an bent it oll to this 'ere funny shaype. Oi rukkin eel get ricketts. Na, wat yer think to't all then? Oim turrifoid.

Oi am, Sir, Yorumble Survent
Jack's woif, Mary

Dear Mary,

Your son, as far as I can divine, has been making attempts upon the construction of a Sandwich. For this instinct of good pedigree he should be held aloft. It is a most excellent way with bread. Indeed nothing accords better with an Adam fireplace and a party at Quadrille than this triangular food of Earls. None the less, I am delivered of a sharp fear that the results of your son's labours to date, are, in all probability, folded, dented and more or less rectangular items, and therefore quite inedible to polite society. So I will endeavour to fall into an account of its edible, equilateral construction.

As with everything in this world there is but one way to proceed. A loaf of unquestionable whiteness, having a yeast of temperate character, should be severed at two millimetres from its ending. The crust, of course, will have been removed by the servants and taken away to some distant place. Sawing with a keen knife must be strictly perpendicular and should avoid at all costs the construction of a doorstep, even such as Mr Adam might take pride in. This procedure is to be repeated along with a priming of butter. At this stage I cannot but look upon a level application of Addison's Relish as the next and most rewarding step.

This tasteful filling comes in three varieties: plover, snipe and woodcock. I must not here omit to say that these birds have a special calling to fill Sandwiches, and the crust – with a piece of bacon rind hung from a hemisphere of coconut – should be recycled to them alone. However, it may happen, dear reader, to gainsay this important facet of their breeding, that other wretched feathered interlopers will presume upon the crust. They are best picked off with a blunderbuss at once. The best houses will be found to retain 'little men'solely for this purpose. A joining of the spread surfaces should now be effected, from which resultant rectangle, four two-tiered triangles may be systematically excised. Each Sandwich, on a pair of scales, should not compute more than the weight of one silken glove, if it is to be acceptable to elderly guests with weak wrists or to persons for some other reason of a fragile disposition. It must finally deserve our most serious attention that a Sandwich is automatically flawed if there be any imprint of human finger or thumb, and that in whatever circumstances of enthusiasm or haste the preparer might find herself, flipping and swatting actions with the human palm are unthinkable.

In regard to the consumption of a Sandwich, I cannot forbear to mention that the nasal organ should never protrude itself between the pasted layers of bread, for even the most admiring inspection. Likewise, one should on no account nurture the ambition to cope with a Sandwich in one mouthful, as people have found to their cost, and to the discomfort of those they are with, that the initial jaw actions necessary to both speech and breath are such as can induce the mouth to reveal its contents, patches to dislodge themselves and wigs and head-dresses to shift alarmingly. On a point of etiquette, whenever the host should indicate that a different flavour of Sandwich has arrived, guests will be expected to pick their teeth and rinse their mouths in the bowls provided.

To continue on a matter of health, it has been found that any manner of Sandwich if soaked for two days in a compound of vinegar, peat and tadpoles will serve to ward off the smallpox, or fried in pig's liver with beetroot for three minutes, will dispel the gout in twelve months, loosen joints and prevent hiccups. For my own part, I know not whether the ancients knew of this curative property in a Sandwich, yet I believe they knew what a Sandwich was. Did not Homer's Odysseus say to his friends in the wooden house, when peckishness prevailed?

'Panis mutatis mutandis magnum opus est.'

And as I find it mentioned in Pindar's Ode, did not Jason survey the seas from the prow of the Argos wondering which way to go for the Golden Fleece, 'ovum inter pane' – with an Egg Sandwich?

In conclusion, Madam, I trust that your son will draw no small encouragement from such classical precedents as these, in whatever of future work he will undertake with the Sandwich, having, might I hope, taken some heed of your present corre-spondent, who is pleased to be,

Yours, within Reason,
Joseph Addison

While Sir Richard Steele and Joseph Addison were covering the syllabus of Essential Decencies and

Advanced Social Manners, a fifty-one year old printer decided that he was in charge of preventing sex before marriage. Not a class of man who immediately occur as sexual authorities – and none have really been heard on the subject since – but Richardson was adamant. Having written a book called 'Jim' telling guys not to, that didn't work, he wrote one called 'Pamela' telling ladies not to, which thank God also didn't work, otherwise the island might have folded up. Yet for all that the book was disturbingly popular, and if it was the slightest bit readable today, might be the Au Pair's Bible – telling a maid, as it does, what to do when her master starts putting all the ornaments on the top shelves, changing the lock on her door, and suggesting casually that blowing dust off is a pretty tame reason for leaning over a sideboard. Richardson had simply decided that whatever Moll Flanders and Fanny Hill might have done, Pamela Andrews was not going to do. Quite where he got all his insights into working-class virgins saying 'no' is presumably something he managed to sort out with his wife, for he does show startling knowledge of the human hand. So much so in fact, that when the story was serialised in the national newspapers, the whole nation hung on the outcome. Not that everybody necessarily adored Pamela's hire-purchase path to a matrimonial bed, for when the last chapter arrived Richardson was both mobbed by women with intimate, tactical enquiries and hunted by a lobby of upset gentlemen with rather different views on how his virtue should be rewarded.

While Addison, Steele and Richardson sought to establish a variety of holds on the common body, Dr Johnson undertook a major spring-cleaning between the average set of ears. Thought, before his arrival, had been a rather dusty, untidy area. Now from a strong, high chair at the back of the Turk's Head Coffee House, there issued daily more blasts of Advice than the King had hot frankfurters in a week. Singlehandedly, Dr Johnson became England's answer to the French Academy. People came from all over England to ask him what words meant. And when they did, they would meet James Boswell Esq, poet, lexicographer's mate, direct descendant of Robert Bruce and leading advocate of Corsican Independence, who would usher them in:

BOSWELL. 'Next, please.' And there entered a woman with a blue stocking who belaboured Dr Johnson above an hour for his definition of the word 'Tongue'. Throughout her speech Johnson seemed to brood until a muffled, squelching sound indicated that his head had come to rest upon two large dumplings in his dinner plate. Seeing their adjacent position confirmed my opinion that Dr Johnson had moved them there for that purpose. Fancying the good doctor to be no longer with us, I hastened to suggest to our guest that we should no longer be with him and that half an hour upstairs with my tooled edition of Pepys would be an exhilarating diversion, when a portentous sloshing of gravy indicated to me that Johnson was awake. JOHNSON. 'Tongue, Madam, is a French word, and it is feminine.' And then our conversation turned, I know not how, to a one-sided comparison of Edinburgh with Sodom, Dr Johnson's declared intention to rebuild Hadrian's Wall with myself on the other side of it, and an abusive judgement which I had not thought to hear from him before. JOHNSON. 'You, Sir, have the morals of a drunken elk and would do well to study the sobriety of the salmon.' This interview confirmed to me Johnson's great humanity and his very deep understanding of Zoology.

At times, Dr Johnson did not mind having Boswell

around. At other times, the whole thing became a little trying:

DR JOHNSON (*catching his finger in a door*): 'Shit.'
BOSWELL: 'Sir?'
DR JOHNSON: 'You did not hear me, Sir.'
BOSWELL: 'But, Sir, you spoke.'
DR JOHNSON: 'Digit, Sir. Mine. In the door, Sir.'
BOSWELL (*whipping out his notebook*): 'One T in digit, Sir?'
DR JOHNSON: 'One T in digit, Sir.'

Slowly, slowly, Dr Johnson realised what he'd let himself in for. He was going to end up the subject of our first classic biography whether he liked it or not. Boswell was unstoppable.

Dr Johnson would probably have written a lot more if Boswell hadn't been writing down everything he said; but on second thoughts that wasn't such a bad thing now I recall stretches of 'Rasselas'*. The good doctor's forte was indubitably the pronouncement. And with Boswell there, we hear all sorts of things history might never have known. His childhood, for example. An area almost beyond imagination if Boswell hadn't told us how it ended at the age of three with the handing back of his teddy bear:

'Conversation, Sir, is impossible with this gentleman. His knowledge of Virgil is not so much imperfect as non-existent. He neither blinks nor questions, and his only response when I throttle his midriff is indistinguishable. I have done with him, Sir, and there's an end on't.'

Or those final, majestic words: 'Tell the Almighty, Sir, to lay one more place at dinner this night. I am tired of London.'

So as any student can see, the Men of Letters were taking the Age of Reason pretty seriously. Man was being told a thing or two. Drama, meanwhile, was bracing itself for the worst. In 1737, Reason struck.

No plays without a Licence. The conditions pursuant to a successful application for a Licence were set out in Aristotle and any decision reached by the Offices of Logical Tragedy and Sensible Comedy was final. Attempts to influence a Q.E.D. Test would disqualify the play from any further consideration other than how to destroy it.

W. Shakespeare managed to slip through the net, but by no means all of him. 'Twelth Night' became 'Second Night'; Bottom and pals were hoiked out of 'A Midsummer Night's Dream' by the Office of Sensible Comedy and dumped into 'The Comedy of Errors', which was banned anyway. The new reasonable play, 'A Midsummer Night's Debate' reappears as a discussion on the misdemeanours of love, chaired by a local town

* A novel. A young West Indian immigrant's romp through the eighteenth century London of his day. Hailed as the black Tom Jones. An uncharacteristic work.

councillor, Mr Puck, and exhibiting the views of Oberon, Mayor of Athens, on the one hand and Demetrius, Helena and co, representatives of the young people of Greece, on the other. After some genial tooing and froing, the debate reaches a timely climax with the incantation of an agreed text.

Stuck with some of the worst plays on record, Drama retaliated with some of the best actors to date. Mr Garrick, Mr Kemble, Mrs Siddons – they all gave the performances of their lives – but not one of them could persuade the Government into letting them have the original texts, though Mrs Siddons once or twice went close in the wings. The emotional Garrick, whose ghost floats over the trees at Hampton, even built Shakespeare a temple, standing quietly proud on the banks of the Thames, to show him how sorry he was about it all, and would he accept a temple etc? So there it was: plays got worse and worse, actors got better and better, till Drama with one or two substantial exceptions became of merely histrionic significance, reaching rock bottom in the next century with Victorian Melodrama.

Reason was by now advancing so well that Mother Nature was about the only person who didn't expect it to be her turn next. Alas, it was. Gone were the days when she could just rustle up a few flowers, couple of trees, maybe a lawn, perhaps a bit of a path, even throw in a pond and think that's all right, that's a garden. Gone too were those nice young poets, who'd come out at any hour of the night, to tell her how pretty she was, and how good it was just to have a chat. Now if a poet launched out into the garden, it was a formal event. And there was no hope of doing it in the dark. Once he'd gone over a Palladian bridge, past the Gothic ruin, round the pagoda, across the lake, got lost in the maze, doubled back through the orangerie to the pavilion recognising a classical statue from half an hour ago, skirted some parallelogram pom-poms in the rockery, shot past a double-rhomboid hedge straight onto a split trapezium lawn, it was just a matter of a few artificial hills and round a Japanese fish-pond before – of a sudden seeing a flower on a bank. And then, as if acting under orders, he would proceed to serve an Ode.

Ode to a primrose

O thou Primrose aureole!
Ye lights of Albion's banks!
Glowing in shades arboreal,
Ye grow in yellow ranks!
Fresh young Nephew to Dandelion,
Counselled of Phoebus' rays
Save when Silent Night is nigh on
And Nymphs their lyres raise.
Then comes Joy with Trojan zeal
To Dance about thy stem a reel,
Till Wisdom, Friend of Pleasure,
Says 'Excuse Me for a Measure!'
Now Bacchus blue-bell, growing cold,
Feels Envy's dampened hand
And Tarquin's Tulip, erstwhile bold,
Regrets on high to stand!
If aught of Greece thou hast forgot
Then Memory will prevail,
And hope with thee an old fox-trot
Till Learning's Self goes pale!
Hail sweet Primrose! Mortals look!
What a Shrine in verdant nook!
O ye Blades of Guardian Grass
Let no Enormous Cow to pass!

I think we can assume, at best, that these poets left a long trail of very puzzled flowers behind them. Even the brightest primrose would have had trouble recognising itself; and if anything like this hit a common or garden gorse bush the whole thing might just as well have been in Greek. But then not all eighteenth century poems were like something orated to a committee for the Verse Prize, from a rostrum to a room full of wooden chairs, when it's grey and raining outside and probably Wednesday afternoon, the odd twig tapping a window pane to keep you awake or perhaps the occasional interesting cough to provide some alternative line of thought for a while. On the contrary, some eighteenth century Poetry was meant to be memorised and used in daily life. Translations from the Classics, Verse Letters on the Good Life, all were intended to bring Guidance and Knowledge to the man in the cobbled street. And none was keener to grab the common rudder than a 4' 6", twenty-three-year-old Catholic called Alexander Pope – although height is probably immaterial when I reflect that Marmaduke, my eldest, is a good 9' and can barely leave a note for the milkman. Without, that is, three days' notice and intense quiet.

Anyhow, after a short apprenticeship on metricising proverbs, Pope thought he'd have a bash at versifying the *Encyclopaedia Britannica*. Talking excitedly with friends in his Grotto, he explained his vision of 'What oft was taught but ne'er so well compress'd' and rattled off the first ten entries in perfect couplets, not even blinking at Aard-Vark. We pick him up here towards the end of the letter 'A', in the 'Essay on Architecture':

> A little building is a Constructive Thing
> Best done by the Irish and after Spring:
> Since first Ionica, not built in a day,
> Rose temples to hold her folk in sway
> Till latest Baroque, home on every street,
> Plump and pastel, cradles our Lords Effete.
> Tis oft the case with Architects Stout
> That some draw on paper while others Grout!
> So Great PALLADIO, seeking a bridge,
> Feels o'er his stomach to take the ridge,
> And sharp-swollen to Size beyond all Dream
> Imagines a Fortress to cross a stream
> Which Lo, when done, would seem to have a Wing:
> Such does innocent Zephyrus make it swing.
> Here goes a Fret, there a Strut again,
> And Judgement, with PALLADIO, weeps in vain.
> Tears to tears! Sad every bridge to fall!
> Yet some say Curs'd ADAM is worst of all.
> Pompous, daft, poncey, Spurious little tit
> Filthy, horrid, nasty, Onerous little git
> Draw closer reader now, and hear it said:
> Scottish Adam will serve us all – when Dead!

There seems to be some infelicity here. Alexander is having distinctly more than a bash at the *Encyclopaedia Britannica*. Did he go short on breakfast? Did his chair collapse? Or could Palladio be Lord Weymouth, known to have blocked planning permission for a bridge at Twickenham, which meant that Pope had to keep walking to Richmond? Was Robert Adam perhaps that tall visitor from the North who infuriated Pope by giggling at his furniture? Well – whatever – Alexander was a bit prone to wander off the subject and get stuck in.

It is, I suppose, sad for the Augustan Dream that while most Augustans were chasing around between concerts worrying about where the next good conversation was going to come from, Pope was not. Pope was down in his Grotto, high on a stool, silent and surrounded by bodyguards, unfolding Damocles. Dark and dreadful, it rolled across the wall, new names to be added, old ones to be deleted. Without moving a face muscle, Pope pondered who to stitch up next. Rockleigh for that letter without a stamp? Burlington for being boring and treading on the cat? Or Winchester for general attitude?

'Quarrelled with Pope' was the shortest, most terrible sentence in the eighteenth century diary. None, in the whole history of the short sentence, had more shattering consequences – except possibly the highly injudicious 'Sounds great, Eve' of Genesis III, passim. People quaked when they realised what they'd written. Bishops took gin at communion; ten foot sergeant majors had to be helped to the lavatory; peers of the realm changed clubs; even gardeners jotting it down on the back of a fag packet underwent extensive bodily changes. It was almost as if Alexander were, in charge, personally, of the atom bomb. But then he could be memorably rude about you. On a good day, he was so good at satire he was even afraid of himself. No wonder the Council wouldn't let him any nearer London than Twickenham and small surprise that his parents thought it safer to have him educated at home. His contemporaries, for example, were all minor poets – he said. To disagree was to be served up in his next poem. No-one in his right mind would have written this paragraph when Pope was around.

Not surprisingly, Alexander all but woke up the Augustan Dream on his own. His vision of the perfect society as one electrifying scrum of gossip, quarrels, nicknames, letting down of coach tyres and fights, was to say the least rather boisterous. But he was not without certain helpers. By the end of the century the Augustan Dream, after several more nightmares, would be fully awake. Pope might have put the cat among the Augustan pigeons. Swift had tigers for 'em.

Sitting on the left hand of God, in the best tradition of pugnacious Irish clerics, the Dean Swift made it resoundingly clear that he preferred the company of horses or Houyhnhnms as he called them, and writing about broomsticks, but would just about settle for eating Irish kids if the first two alternatives were not available. Dr Johnson, of course, went bonkers at this. But Swift didn't care. P – s on him! As far as he was concerned, society was selfish and smelly to a fault – although he wisely allowed a certain amount of détente with Pope on this one by making out that Lilliput was a nice place for a holiday. As for the rest of humanity, they were just a load of Yahoos – a species delineated in 'Gulliver's Travels' – and believed to be based on Earls Court.

In fact, Swift got so put off by people that he usually spent most of his time in the bath. For him, the scrubbing brush was a d – n sight better than the pen. The world was his oyster with a strong bit of bristle. And preferably eighteen hours a day in which to use it. Women being women, some of them liked this approach, but the Dean maintained adamantly that he was too odd for young women really to fancy. As the years went by, and Dr Johnson cooled off, Swift rarely left the bath at all. Diminishing through cleanliness, defiantly drinking detergent to the end, Jonathan Sw – t eventually disappeared down the Eternal Plughole, being one day returned like us all to that Great Douche in the sky. From his final, dehydrated phase of aquatic excess comes the delirious, autobiographical 'Tale of a Tub'*:

> 'Run the Bath! – THE DEAN is back!'
> 'And Soap! – Enough to wash a Yak!'
> 'He passed through the congregation!'
> 'Oh J★★★s! Get the embrocation!'
> 'Worms, you say, spat against his ear?'
> 'Well, he always did stand too near!'
> 'And left his hat upon a chair?'
> 'No wonder fleas trapeeze his hair!'

* Squeamish students should skip this completely. More robust candidates proceed at their own discretion, should they have any.

'Now up to the room of steam
With brush in hand staggers THE DEAN!
(Armpits beware! And Ears look out!
Fleas, worms feed on! Here comes the rout!)
And then DECANUS starts to rub
From his Navel a brace of Grub!
Before letting fly with a f**t –
To kill 'em in the air! That's Art!
And never once been known to miss
The Dean sees 'em off with a p***!
Then Snot and Vapours! On to Wax!
Great Sanitation grants no pax.
Lux, the bashful Muse, waits below
Soon at Chancres to have a go!
Nits, gnats, vermin! Scurf, slop and silt!
Run, wriggle, ooze! Dissolve and wilt!

Now Father, Son and Holy Ghost
Drown all Parasites in our Host!

Here we must leave the Dean en suite and travel to
the walled garden of an old rectory in Yorkshire to meet
another minister from the emerald isle whose contribution to the Augustan Dream was altogether more
peaceful. He was asleep.

In the bird-sweet balm of his rambling, tangled garden
where golden ragwort drooped its head in the interstices
of the crumbling outer wall and ivy had for centuries
lagged the stable door, only the sound of some drowsy
cow mooing indolently at a rusty lock or an apple plom-
ping down from the espalier to the lawn, could rouse
the Reverend Lawrence Sterne. But when the call to
action came Sterne really could be quite active, pottering
round his garden, drifting through intervals of gentle
cogitation. Moving at a pace well within himself, he
would wonder vaguely whether the breathing habits of
the trout didn't constitute something rather better than
an alternative to drowning. Perhaps not as forthright as
the Roman minnow, and surrendering a good deal in
girth to the Whale of Babylon, but possessed none the
less of quite exemplary gills. A fish one would be happy
to have nibbling one's toes in the Elysian Springs. He

might, then, turn over amiably the possibility of there being a Viking teaspoon somewhere around the bird-bath, where earlier that year his trowel had scooped up the vestiges of a Nordic teapot – much to the delight of the ladies of the local antiquarian society. But then again, a line or two of 'Tristram Shandy' might be in order.

'Tristram Shandy' was Sterne's private dream. For years, he toyed with the idea of writing a novel without a story and perfecting the dash, until, almost without noticing it, 'Tristram Shandy' was finished. In one longer, unswerving digression Sterne brought the dash to its literary peak – if that is – and he'd be the first to admit it – you can actually bring a dash to a peak. It was an odd book. Not even Dr Johnson could explain it. What is in it need not concern us, but all agreed that what Swift had done for the asterisk, Sterne had done for the dash.

All in all, Sterne wasn't displeased with 'Tristram Shandy'. It had occasionally led him to forget an appointment, and at times meant that he didn't perhaps make the best of good fishing weather, but a few nicely cooked London dinners had more or less won him round to the small annoyances of composition. He might try another book.

The Augustan Establishment, meanwhile, hoped he wouldn't. A dash was all right in its own way, but where was the firm story line, the solid moral instruction? After all, if a Reverend couldn't write an improving book in an Age of Reason, who could? Two hundred years later of course, Sterne's exhilarating punctuation, oodles of improbable opinions and narrative amnesia were to enthrone him as something of a high priest – but to the officials of the Augustan Establishment he was to say the least an awkwardly frivolous recumbent.

Yet, unfortunately, there came to pass an horde of novelists who celebrated the perception that life was a rollicking shambles. Englishmen weren't going to be Romans! Fielding, Defoe and Smollett had obviously decided just to enjoy the eighteenth century anyway. Don't stop if there's another bucket of cabbage and ale;

don't stint if you've got a good heart, and there's still a barrel of port in the kitchen. Don't be selfish with your body if there's a generous-hearted wench to hand. Anyway, she's probably got a thousand guineas, and a favourably ailing uncle. Novels like this were generally written with the hope that they would be filmed at high speed with an endless background of harpsichord music e.g.

The History and Somewhat Remarkable Life of Ned Nefarious

Found one morning after a thunderstorm, in a wheel barrow on Squire Hogwash's front lawn, Ned is welcomed into the household. Fondled by Mrs Bucket, tutored by Shoesqueak, and adored by the Squire's daughter Julie, Ned grows into a fine lad of good heart. The rescuing of a drowning beagle more than compensates for an earlier incident of low trousers and high spirits behind the potting shed, so that Ned finds himself promised to the beautiful Julie and made heir to the Hogwash Estate. But, before time, Ned is on his travels after cooked evidence by the lecherous and hypocritical Shoesqueak suggests that Ned is the connecting factor between the disappearance of pigs from the Hogwash Estate and the inability of a local hostelry to supply anything but pork pies.

Making his way to London, his fortunes at a low ebb, Ned is accosted on the A371 outside of Wincanton by the one-elbowed, one-ankled Captain Backfire who persuades him over the German frontier to Bad Bratwurst and into the War of Ludwig's Lederhosen, where the good Captain loses both knee-caps in a duel with Otto von Mettelhelmet, whereupon Ned distinguishes himself by selling all the Captain's superfluous shoes and departing for the West Indies. Posing as doctor on board a ship bound for Lisbon, Ned retails surgical spirit to the increasingly jolly tars until they change course for the Caribbean where the irrepressible Ned leads them into a Spanish port and generously surrenders the ship and entire crew in exchange for the Governorship of Tobago where he settles down to a life of growing sugar cane and 'fixing' cricket matches till an amorous interview with the Spanish Ambassador's wife obliges him to leave, under a crate of bananas on the next ship.

Landing back at Liverpool, Ned decides to give himself a summer season round the changing-room lockers at Bath. Busying himself in the romantic spa town, Ned has the good fortune to be befriended by the whimsical and hygienic Beau Loo, who for a modest fee, secures him a place in the employment of the near-insatiable Lady Cobblegarter with whom duties back in London rapidly take a turn for the physical, so far above and beyond the rigours of mere coach maintenance that it is soon all Ned can do to hang on at the back. A deep pothole, early one morning, sees Ned finally drop from the back of the coach. Lying on the street, he is picked up by William Brimfire, a pale Methodist, who astride his faithful donkey Barabbas, rehabilitates Ned, teaching him all the new tunes, eliminating Vodka and Spanish Fly from his every drink, giving him a few hints on preaching and patiently waiting for the day when Ned feels he is ready to go into holy orders. That day never comes. One rainy night at Tunbridge Wells an experienced young serving wench subjects Ned's sanctity to tests which archdeacons would fail, and she assured him, often had.

Speeding towards London with the hot Fanny Smolders, Ned ponders anew what sources of revenue are available to them. Pickpocketing wins their unanimous approval – as does the verdict of 'guilty' with the courtroom which eventually consigns them to Newgate. On their way to the gallows Ned and Fanny wonder at their former circumstances in life, and are beginning to notice some strange similarities, when Lady Cobblegarter rushes from the crowd to halt the execution. Fanny, it transpires, is her daughter and they have not seen each other since the day a press-gang removed her from her cot outside a hostelry in Wiltshire. There is a son as well, but she has not seen him since he was exiled from Squire Hogwash's Estate many years ago. It is then that Lady Cobblegarter, née Bucket, explains the money left to her in the Hogwash will, and her subsequent marriage into easy circumstances. Ned, at that point, feeling in distinctly uneasy circumstances, steps forward. The recognition scene that follows gathers momentum until Lady Cobblegarter announces that the beautiful Julie Hogwash is expected to arrive on a visit that afternoon. Ned is delighted – and when they meet they rediscover, in a touching scene, all their old love for one another. Ned proposes, when Julie has finished telling him all about Uncle Hogwash's legacy, and they settle down together to a life of serene happiness, with Ned putting prize marrows into the local flower show every year and walking every Sunday across the fields to church with his sons Jack and Humphrey.

As if certain gentlemen hadn't already done enough, the Augustan Dream of an Age of Reason was just about to get its final, rousing prod. Just when it needed a good volume of sermons or a novel of sound, moral deduction, poets one by one, began to fall off their perch.

Macpherson. Highland schoolmaster. Colour of eyes at beginning of term, throstle blue. Experienced difficulty understanding that he was not a third century Gaelic warrior called Ossian, but master in charge of carpentry. Confined after leading attack on cricket hut, laying waste to school boat-house, and publishing inflammatory translations of Gaelic poems which never existed. Whereas, Tommy Chatterton, 'the wonderful boy', rather overdid that phase of adolescence when one wants to spend the summer hols in a monastery, by proclaiming himself to be a fifteenth century monk. Disabused of this notion by everybody who got to know him, Chatterton, alias Father Rowley, is widely thought to have draped himself across a bed and taken the bitter cup. What is not generally known is that he got better.

Christopher Smart didn't. Set off to find himself in religion, got lost, and wound up not even being able to give you the change from a packet of fags. Blake.

Blake wouldn't have known what a packet of fags was. Personally I think this was just as well when you consider that he heard colours, saw with his ears, smelt with his eyebrows and depended upon his fingers for balance – but you mustn't say things like that in front of some of my colleagues.* For them, opening a volume of Blake is equivalent to entering a church. For not only was he politically reliable but mad as a March hare, which, artistically, makes him pretty hot property. In fact, throw in TB and syphilis and Shakespeare might be wondering why he even bothered.

However, all this is distracting us from the main problem with Blake which is to know what on earth he's talking about. Normally one needs some help with this one. This is why critical books on Blake are always dedicated: 'TO MARVIN DOPPELBERGER, who helped me understand Blake'. To start with, Blake's language makes Arawak a two-day linguaphone course, so I'd suggest my own trilogy of 'Teach Yourself Blake', 'Advanced Blake' and 'Conversational Blake' as a linguistic lead-in. But then there's still the trouble of what's

* Nor certain of my students. Jack's paint pot has already made it apparent to the saddle of my bicycle that any criticism of Blake is 'totally unacceptable'. Not wishing to spend another Sunday morning with a bucket of turps, I managed to persuade him that Blake's desire to build Jerusalem with a bow and arrow was embryonic Zionist Imperialism and no less culpable than his racist victimisation of the prolific Mills family next door to him in Peckham Rye, namely 'these dark Satanic Mills'. Mercifully, he seemed quite pleased with all this. Alas, too pleased. The Faculty now has to cope with 'Racist Zionist' on the door of the downstairs ladies loo.

it all about anyway? So faced with the unusual double question of how is he saying whatever he is saying, one naturally posits a second question: wasn't there an easier way of doing all this?

The truth of the matter is – not if you were Blake. After all, anyone who can hear a sunset, bristle his eyebrows in front of a bonfire and see sideways, is more than likely to be carried singing to the grave, having left his cat to the florist. And Blake's ears saw more than most – e.g. God outside Sainsbury's at eleven-thirty whence, according to him (small 'h'), they went off together to look for a pair of sandals, until it was time for Blake's other appointments – an afternoon at Whipsnade with Daniel, a bit of early evening wind-surfing with Jonah, before a chaotic night round the clubs with Joshua and sharing a late-night bag of chips with Ezekiel on the corner of Tottenham Court Road.

Blake's poetry duly has an element of the street guide in it. Not, of course, that it should ever be consulted for this reason. 'The Fields from Walthamstow to Camberwell' wouldn't get you very far:

> The fields from Walthamstow to Camberwell
>> Stretch wide and long in meadows green
> Children run and play in innocent ease
>> And Urk advances quite unseen.
>
> Stand up West Bromwich Albion!
>> Jerusalem! The Mole is here!
> Bold Urk breaks the jealous surface
>> And pops into the air an ear.
>
> Past go the hooves of the Golden Giraffe
>> Destroying all the Flowers
> Up goes the Mole to the top of the Tree
>> And sits up there amazed for hours.
>
> Then I went to the Old Kent Road
>> And saw what I had never seen:
> The Golden Head and Hooves, at speed,
>> Bobbing, cursing and digging keen.
>
> The fields from Walthamstow to Camberwell
>> Stretch wide and long in meadows green
> Children run and play in innocent ease
>> And Urk returns quite unseen.

Blake at once is posing us with problems. We have to accept that Jerusalem is the capital of England, and roamed both by giraffes – or at the very least, a bloody great big golden one – and tree-climbing moles – or perhaps just a sort of one-off tree-climbing mole. However, once re-adjusted the student is then well on the way to understanding 'The Fields from Walthamstow to Camberwell', for what is really happening is that Urk, an amoral, pre-Judaic Babylonian Force of Untidiness, Chaos and LSD, has enticed the Mole representing Abysmal Disinterest, Frustration and Potholing to pull out his front claws to make the effort to Jerusalem where he is further persuaded to shoot up a tree, thereby relinquishing his essential Moleness, just as the Giraffe, a symbol of Gradual Curiosity with an emphasis on height, Exhilaration, Soul and the Artist, is also sufficiently under Urk's influence to be seen digging a burrow in the Old Kent Road, thereby turning his back on all that the 'Songs of Inexperience' should have taught him about Giraffehood. 'Flowers' incidentally represent the agency of Eternal Hope, while 'green' denotes a quality of blackness and Sleep. In the next poem, 'Giraffe' stands for Suet Pudding and the Mole reappears as Not Having Shaved That Morning, but this is all by the way.

All by the way, too, was the thought that there was anyone about who was prepared to be reasonable any more. The French were all over the shop, having more revolutions than there were public holidays available to celebrate them. The Americans of course had already over-reacted and were declaring war on each other, whilst in England howls of derision greeted words like 'therefore' and 'because'. And you could get hit for saying 'hence'. Even the Earl of Chesterfield's son wedged a dustbin up against the front door for his old man's letters. The simple fact was that by the end of the eighteenth century you couldn't get a bloke to be reasonable any more. After one hundred years of thinking they all wanted to be passionate. Passion was in the air, passion was free, passion was in the mountains, passion raged. Race to the windows, pop your buttons and look hopeless was what it was all about. And so it was – with the moving spectacle of young, starry-eyed mathematicians fighting their way into tight, red trousers and giving their locks one last, diabolical rake for luck that the Augustan Dream of an Age of Reason could be said to have ended.

Dorothy's Diary

The mood of explosive Passion which tore through the realm, following the collapse of Reason, made everybody feel a good ten years younger – and look at least twenty years older. For the Romantic Movement was no mere insinuation of an elbow, encurling of a toe or straightening of a finger, but a tremendous erotic explosion which engulfed revolutions, poetry, drugs, love and Nature. Quite a handful, as even the randiest scholar will admit. Yet, incredibly, five people managed to be more Romantic than all the rest of us together. Wordsworth, a north-country botanist, keen on children and simple folk; Coleridge, a strung-out vicar's son prone to fits of improbable theory and stories with a sea-bird interest; Shelley, a lunatic; Keats, not a lunatic but you wouldn't exactly want him doing the baby-sitting either; Byron, a wicked lord.

Still, anticipating Mrs Dale by over a hundred and fifty years, Dorothy Wordsworth has left us an everyday story of life with the Romantics. But before giving extracts from her revealing diary, let us briefly preview the characters to appear and the attitudes they shared.

It seems that five young rebels had all come up to Dope Cottage at Meregrass in 1803, to indulge themselves in poetry, drugs, love and Nature. This is the famous Romantic Revival because they often had to be brought round with smelling salts, brisk walks, sermons and soda water. Naturally they didn't live very long – and all looked alike, wearing unbuttoned shirts, long hair, wild eyes and being pale and ill. They all despised towns, science, parents, classical music, long woollen underpants, bank managers and logic, tending to faint, vomit, run into the garden or burst into tears if these words were ever used in their presence. On the other hand, they were easily excited by the Continent where there were revolutions and scenery, tending to flush with joy, flare the nostrils and dive at the sofa and end up across a flattened lampshade, hopelessly blissed, if these words were even whispered.

It is unfortunate that we don't know more about Dorothy. She is without doubt the greatest unpublished housewife in our literature. Still, I suppose we can guess that it can't have been easy looking after all those Romantics – and, at times, a bit tempting? Her diary does indeed leave unanswered a few big ones. With brother William at Goslar in Germany during the early winter of 1809. Did they? When Coleridge late one night at Brydal Mount sat in his underwear and explained Pantisocracy to her, the wind whistling in the hollies. This incident ends abruptly in the diary and the evidence suggests that there was a struggle over the missing page. And the number of times she nearly drowned in the lake reflects suspiciously on the efficacy of Byron's swimming lessons.

But enough of that and let us attend to what she does have to say. We take up her diary in March 1803 at Dope Cottage. The abuse detonated by Wordsworth and Coleridge in the desperately serious 'Lyrical Ballads' has acted as a rallying call to the other three Romantics to come up to Meregrass without delay. William, Coleridge and Dorothy await their arrival.

FRIDAY, MARCH 13TH. A very wet morning. Don't think I'll put the washing out to dry. William lying in the vegetable patch, composing. Coleridge at the sink peeling a large purple fungus and pressing me to eat it with him. I took issue saying it was his last, whereupon he replied that it would be if I didn't share it with him. C. very intense for the rest of the afternoon. Spent four hours ironing a sock. While I languished in the pantry. C. locked it, thought it was the front door. Late tea. Freezing night.

SATURDAY, MARCH 14TH. Poor William! Found him still in the vegetable patch this morning. His face a wonderful blue, azure as the skies. Had to chip him out of the ice and put him to bed. Coleridge buried his nose into one of De Quincey's letters, sniffed deeply and wrote 'Frost at Midnight'. William not amused.

SUNDAY, MARCH 15TH. A beautiful morning. And three letters! They're arriving today! William asked me to stay and greet them and went off fishing. C. very busy, digging up his plants, chopping and rolling them into long paper cylinders. At ten o'clock, there was a fearful coughing from outside the front door. I opened it. 'Hullo, I'm Keats. Is this Meregrass? Thank Christ!' and fell into the porch. C. put him to bed with a few pills. Heard William returning at 12 o'clock. Deep in argument.'– It would be impossible for me to concur

with your suggestion that I was fishing with anything less than the most serious intentions. Furthermore, I had exceeded all my usual bounds of patience . . .' '–Ayup 'avvyer don? they say in these parts, I believe.' '– Moreover it is most unwelcome to have to stress to you the disastrous wreckage of my schemes which was occasioned by your tumultuous passage in the water. Therefore . . .' '– Bloody silly place to be fishing. And what about my trunks? A pretty mess your damned hook made of them.' Whereupon William strode into the house, and introduced me in tones of cold dignity to Lord Byron. So these were the proud, flashing eyes of dark secrets which the ladies of London society melted before. Those were the stern brows of the man who openly admitted to being famous in the morning. And I guiltily own to a certain catching of my breath when he spoke his first words to me: 'Any good with a needle and thread?' I replied in the affirmative, though I dearly felt like saying 'Pass'. And then. He spoke again. 'My apologies to you, Mr. Wordsworth, and I shall repay your kind sister for her repairs by making her amphibious'. He went straightaway to his room, and I fell to the nearest dictionary and wept in confusion.

Gave William a boiled mutton chop for lunch, and he returned to his fishing with a warm glow. C. lying on the sofa in 'cosmic Zugswang'. No sign of Keats or his Lordship. Heard William returning at five o'clock, most irate: '– Strange fits of Passion have I known, but truly vertiginous heights rose in me when you, with no little commotion and appalling accuracy, rowed straight through the centre of my shoal. In the name of God, do you understand a word I'm saying?' '– Sublimely. My soul is an enchanted boat, swept along by winged oars, kissed by the waves, inspired by gentle Zephyrus. Through snow and lightning on the roof of the world . . .' '– Yes, yes. Let's go in.' William spoke rather curtly. 'This is Shelley', and went up to rest. Showed Shelley to his room, losing him a few times on the way as he paused to observe cobwebs and icicles. Upon reaching his room at last he spoke: 'Pray, blithe spirit, what was that on the sofa?' 'Coleridge' I answered. 'Oh', said he, speaking very slowly and fingering a dead leaf, 'Coleridge . . . then . . . I'm here. Say it again for me.' 'Coleridge', I repeated. 'O World! O Life! O Time! Hail to thee, O Coleridge. Pinnacled in the mist that around thee lies, blazened in the dawn of the morning skies an eagle, O an eagle among tits . . .' At which point I sought my room in haste.

MONDAY, MARCH 16TH. A glorious morning and every-body down early to breakfast. Terrific argument over porridge about where everybody was going to compose. William, as landlord, got the path; Shelley bagged the copse from which he proposed to break out at intervals composing on the burst. Byron was blowing up some rubber thing in the corner and looking indifferent; Keats insisted that sensations of an opposite nature should be present for his inspiration but agreed that there didn't have to be a particular place for this to happen; C. reluctant to commit himself at this juncture. Peeped through the window at mid-morning. All at the height of their powers.

A full table at supper. All enjoyed the scrambled moorhen, except K. who mysteriously vomited. Shelley sat in the corner, a little apart, with a hazelnut and a glass of dew, talking to William's sideboard. C. brought us all together with great numbers of his paper cylinders requesting our willing suspension of disbelief as it was very good stuff bought from an old sailor who guaranteed 'it stoppeth one of three'. Well, it started us all right.

Keats proclaimed his support for the working classes of Greece with 'Ode on a Grecian Ern', while Byron deliberately infuriated William with a poem about Birmingham. C. beneath clouds of smoke tried to explain Pantisocracy to us, but gave up and invited us instead to declare U.D.I. at Meregrass. Shelley thought that Padua might be a bit warmer – pointing out that we would be better placed to take over the world in a country where citrus fruits grew naturally. There was then a long pause while everybody tried to understand what Percy was talking about, until Keats, flushed, agreed that he'd rather be on the Continent – a remark which at once launched all five poets at the sofa, who, of course, missed and completely destroyed my lampshade. Their bodies like a pile of twisted branches, their eyes like blue flowers in milk, opened to each other imploring climactic release. 'Picardie' whispered Keats, as if blowing a feather from a child's face. 'Provence' countered Byron. 'The Caspian Sea' droned William. 'Afric's golden sands' bawled Coleridge. And they were off: 'The

Pyrenees', 'The Greek Islands', 'The Mezzogiorno', 'Inner Mongolia', 'Und ruhig fliesst der Rhein', 'Mont Blanc', 'The Sahara', 'We've had that once', 'The Bosphorus', 'The Mouth of the Ganges', 'Gay Paris', "Get off Byron", 'The Bay of Biscay', 'Cloud Cuckoo Land', 'The White Cliffs of Dover', 'The Pennines', 'Meregrass' – and they were all back safely.

Weary from their travels at long last, they all made for the stairs while I put the room straight again. Emptying rubbish into the dustbin I paused to look up at the night sky giving way to the early dawn. It was as if the Future, shy on the misty hill-tops knew that those young men upstairs were on the verge of cracking open all its secrets.

TUESDAY, MARCH 17TH. What a day! William rose refreshed, consumed a bucket of porridge and walked to Scotland. C. sat on a window ledge 'getting the feel of an albatross'. Poor Shelley spent the morning writhing and groaning in a corner of the lounge from which I erroneously assumed that he was having a poem. 'Just wind' he said. However, when I thought Percy's wind was finished, and that at last I might be able to have a quiet moment with Byron's trunks, Keats threw up his work. O Joy, what a lovely thought! He was going to explain the notes of the nightingale to me! I quickly put the supper on, moved Percy to another part of the house and raced back to the fireside. But, oh, what anguish lay ahead of me! K. experienced such a barrage of hiccups and whooping cough that I couldn't really make much of the nightingale. We were still, I think, on the lower branches when William's momentum brought him through the front door, over the sofa and into the lounge wall.

WEDNESDAY, MARCH 18TH. Saw Byron at breakfast, splendid in his rubber suit, drinking mint tea out of a skull. Said he could do a magpie in bed with a robin if I was interested. Didn't know where to look, so chucked a newspaper at him and told him he was awful. And then suddenly it happened, arriving like a thunderbolt across the draining board. He gave me one of his looks. All proud, distant and defiant, the face of a man who had fought tigers, strangled crocodiles and duffed hippos, and all to keep a macabre tryst with a dying woman in the heart of a blazing jungle. I clutched for the tablecloth as my knees started to go. If he spoke now. I was gone. 'Is this the only newspaper you've got?', and I hit the deck. Full moon. Baying noises from Shelley's room. Heard K. wheezing 'Shut up Shelley. Romantic fool.'

THURSDAY, MARCH 19TH. All up at the crack of noon today, except S. A quiet day really. Gave the wheelbarrow a good old clean, dusted Coleridge and made a huge Passion Fruit Pie for tonight. At seven William sounded the gong, having to make the usual excursion to Coleridge's bedside for a closer and more multiple rendering. William throughout supper jollied us along with pitchers of his daffodil wine which Byron thought very conducive to animating strains in company. At which point K., alas, vomited over Percy. And Pandemonium broke out. B. tried to comfort P. but 'The sod scarce heaved' was little comfort as the sod – William's highest term of praise -- had indeed heaved. And rather well. So much so that C. put a drink on Percy's head thinking it was the floral settee.

Things got going a bit after that. K. recovered and spotted a linnet, pointing it out to us in great excitement. And sure enough, outside the winndow on a branch, there was a linnet. William was almost beside himself with emotion:

> O Linnet, sitting in the tree,
> Tho' tis late and dark and very cold;
> Tho' I am full thirty-six years old,
> Whilst thou art barely two years old,
> Hast thou no grand thought of me?
> For this I apprehend and hold it true
> Feather-fram'd Wisdom runs deepest in you:
> Transcending human lot without despair
> Thou know'st the elements of Duty in it;
> Sober thou art to gloom beyond compare,
> Cognisant of Universal Limit.
> And thou shalt have thy daily bread from me,
> Who ne'er till now saw comfort in a tree.

'William, brilliant! Bravo!', I cried, and just what I put in my diary last week.'

'Recollected as a glandular process in tranquillity and transmuted into great verse, Dorothy.'

'Of course, William. Yes.'

Slowly, William lowered his arm and put away his thumb. The sighting was over. He looked exhausted. 'Well', said K., 'if there's no more, can I have a go?' 'Your linnet, Mr. Keats', replied William. K. nervously contorted his fingers, put pepper on his tongue, took a draught of cold claret and broke into beautiful poetry:

> Deep in the cruel silence of Arctic seas
> Wan gulls circle, plummet, fall to their knees–
> Yet, O hard-billed Dryad, thou dost also know,
> Forlorn on tip-toe, to night's frozen cheek,
> That eye-lids heavy with white-fingered snow
> And feet like granite, make it hard to speak:
> But soft! – drink thou this winter-warming ale,
> And pourthy bird-song down the vale.

I was by now in a state of high agitation, and Percy was weeping openly. 'You have treated us Mr. Keats' said William, with quiet solemnity. 'True friends. Too kind' said K. choking. Silence fell over the room, with only the occasional sound of a body coming to terms with itself. At nine thirty C. stood up. He felt it was incumbent upon him to advise us of his contribution, during the course of which he proposed to use 'nose rhyme' and suggest alternative powers in the universe. We waited, with a sense of new frontiers, as C. opened his eyes wide and delicately flared his nostrils:

> On they travel, short of linseed,
> Linnets, far from home of moss,
> Till at sea edge, they eat seaweed
> Turning one and all to albatross.

'Very sound, Coleridge, very sound' applauded William. 'Yes, linseed and seaweed are pretty close' enthused Keats, 'what do you say Byron?' 'Never smelt an albatross Johannis old fruit', and put his head back into the crossword which I noticed he'd picked up as soon as he'd seen William's thumb going into the air. Feeling there was safety in numbers, I asked his Lordship what he had to offer us. Without even raising his head from the paper, he yawned. And then looked straight at me:

> From the lounge only a linnet I see,
> Yet tutored deeply in philosophy!

And he'd done it again – confusing my defences, upsetting my security, making me doubt all my values, drawing me into his world where I understood little, yet strangely yearned for everything. 'More tea, Byron?' I stammered, there being no other discernible reaction in the room. He didn't reply. Percy, on the other hand, was beginning to make incredible noises, going redder and redder, starting to bounce in his chair, and to all appearances, on the verge of some explosion. Thinking to ease Percy's difficulties, I offered him a glass of punch. He put this carefully on the table and the worst seemed past. However, of a sudden, he leapt out of his seat, tearing off his shirt:

Voices of phantoms of domes of linnets,
Child ghosts hovering! O away with me!
Deep wild forests flailing, thou know'st the way!
Treacherous flaming bosoms blazing free,
Jealous of the moon and bones of water,
Death and birth fraught with travelling windsway,
Surpassing lofty devotion cradled . . .

William at this point grabbed Percy, and Byron talked him down. 'It's all right Percy. We're all here. And anyway, it's flown off.' He can be so understanding at times. And he was right too. Our linnet was gone. Phrases and words rang in my ears all night as I reflected that that little bird, without ever knowing it, had been immortalised.

FRIDAY, MARCH 20TH. A lovely morning. The mountains laughing. And moss cheerful in the crags. William off to measure a rhododendron, C. talking fluent German to the postman. Byron up earlier than usual and hurriedly feeding the lounge fireplace with the morning newspapers. 'Oh, The Meregrass Bugle', I cried, seeing the headlines disappearing into the flames – 'For the First Time: The Truth About The Real Lord Byron, his

cousin, a goat, Steeple Bumpstead Choir and a cricket bat'. 'We're not having that in the house', stormed Byron, 'bloody investigative journalism.' Assuring him that I didn't a see thing, and discreetly trying to put the fire out, I suggested that he might like to go hunting. He seemed pleased with the idea. Took his 'Shelley pod' with him for company. 4.30 . . . and still trying to work out how the goat is involved. 4.31, kitchen window blown in. 4.32, frantic ringing of doorbell, another explosion, and something off the roof. C. now took the initiative, crawling to the front door with a white hand-kerchief and a French dictionary – only to find himself looking at B's feet: 'We can all thank bloody Apollo here for that little lot.'

SATURDAY, MARCH 21ST. Coleridge brought me an early morning cup of tea. Don't remember anything else.

SUNDAY, MARCH 22ND. 'Stroth as I live. William is considering holy matrimony! He vows never to have seen handwriting such as my friend Mary's and now that she has shown him her fair copies, he feels it is simply a matter of time before he will ask her to cope with his calligraphy. C. already preparing his speech, amidst much rejoicing in the house. Almost crooning with happiness, I go off to find the glazier in Heatherbracken. Returning at midday with a celebratory partridge, I discover the mood in the house to have changed alarmingly:

'RENT?', said Byron. 'My room hasn't even got a shower in it.'

'Three and fourpence would also cover wear and tear', William pointed out.

'Rent?' asked Shelley. 'What's that?'

'At three and fourpence, you, Mr Shelley, are getting off lightly.'

'No heating in my room', argued Keats. 'Haven't got three and fourpence anyway.'

'I fully appreciate the situation in which a young poet will find himself. You can owe it to me.'

'Well. I'm off' said Byron. 'I'm fed up with mint cake, the weather and no women. I fancy a moonlit gondola with a plump half-pissed contessa. What say you, Percy-poo?'

'Tyranny, Mr Wordsworth, will not enslave me, nor rent reduce my spending. I intend to follow the cuckoo to Africa.'

'Well said, Percy', hooted Byron. 'Let's pack for Italy. It's on the way.'

'Do any of you nurture the intention of further sojourn? Mr Keats?' asked William.

'Perforce, Mr Wordsworth, the lure of the Mediterranean is upon me. My nostril craves the moist scent of wild mimosa and my ears ring with the cicada. And I need a tan. Oh, fancy it' said Keats.

'Imagine it', corrected Coleridge.

'Fuck it' said Byron. 'Let's go.'

And within the hour William, Coleridge and myself were out gathering sticks in uneasy silence, watching in the distance as the Meregrass Arrow sped away through the dales with Byron, Shelley and Keats. I wondered, aimlessly cutting the rope on a well-bucket, whether I should ever see him again.

I don't know whether my colleagues believe in this sort of thing or not, but Dorothy Wordsworth was to see Byron again. And Wordsworth and Coleridge saw Shelley and Keats. For after an interval of eighteen years, during which there was correspondence (although usually in the form of last demands from William), a florid plea arrived for the inhabitants of Meregrass to come to Venice without delay. Of the journey of Byron, Shelley and Keats to Italy, there is not much to relate.

We take up Dorothy's account in Venice, though she'd filled a book before they got to Derby. It is August, 1821, at the Palazzo Solo Poco Acqua Minerale.

WEDNESDAY, AUGUST 1ST. 'Oh B. this is lovely' I cried, as the water filled my shoes in the lounge, 'but how is K. getting on?' 'Marvellous, Dotty. Learnt the Italian for "rat" and has the situation well under control.' William strode in with his pink legs, shorts and Wellington boots.

'Willy, you old Lake Poet. Come sta? No daffodil wine here I'm afraid but some quite nice stuff they make out of grapes.' 'So I am informed', quipped William. 'And where's old C.?' rioted Byron. 'Party wouldn't be complete without him.' 'Mr Coleridge', replied William, 'is under the impression that Venice is full of plesiosaurs, so we left him the addresss and time with which to furnish himself with a fuller study of the matter. 'Good thinking, Willy. Now, for the time being, get to your hammocks and we'll wade out for dinner tonight.' 'Hasta la pasta', I joked, feeling quite Dotty.

Everyone at pasta tonight. Oh Italy is a wonderful place. I feel four years old and on the pill. Percy, full of fun, recounts fiasco at the frontier. Apparently, B. and K. had to leave him there while he tried to explain what 'the unacknowledged legislator of mankind' was doing in his passport. The customs man complained that Italy didn't need any more of these, but if Percy had 4000 lire he could change his plea to shoe salesman and be off down the autostrada in two minutes. Percy agreed; but then the cambio man had gone into Austria for the afternoon. Well, not to worry, did Percy have any foreign loose change that would fit the coffee machine? He did? Right. O.K. On your way. Never before have I witnessed such an immoderate display of laughter from William: he came right out of himself, ordering Sambuca galore and singing Rule Britannia in his new leather boots before telling the waitress to add the date to the bill. Coleridge delivered himself at great length on the plesiosaur and luminous yo-yos. And as for K., I hve never seen him so well. He despatched the first course without even a burp. At last, back to our hammocks and all swinging above the water without a care.

THURSDAY, AUGUST 2ND.　　?

FRIDAY, AUGUST 3RD. Woken at dawn by the clashing of steel and cracking of pistols. I go downstairs and find B. charging a blown-up photo of a Turk, although by all appearances B. has won. 'Ciao, Dotty' he called from the other side of the Turk, 'just warming up for the

125

Greeks. There's squid risotto in the fridge. Might give Coleridge something to think about. Otherwise it's coffee and moon rocks. See you all later anyway. Show Contessa Friscinoccas down here if she calls. Havvat Mustapha!' And I left, warmed by the sight of a man with so much to believe in. Found Percy at midday in a windcheater, poring over a map. 'First Prize is £500', he explained. 'For what?' I asked. 'Winning the Round Italy Off-Shore Dinghy Race' he shouted, clapping his hands together and jumping up and down in his bobble hat. So much so in fact that I nearly missed C. leaving by the back door with a harpoon. I shouldn't really have let him go. Bumped into K. this afternoon. He favours Rome as his next stop. Fanny hasn't seen the Colisseum yet, and K. feels that this, followed by a good siesta, could do the trick. And there's always the Vatican if that doesn't work. We turn to discussing Fanny in a general sort of way, when William arrives, breathless and desperate to enlist our help. C. is two piazzas away, and pulling towards him a sinking and increasingly noisy plesiosaur, intent upon proving to bystanders that those bounty hunters out there had nothing to do with it. The dwindling occupants looking only too eager to give an account of themselves upon land, we remove C. with a sense of great urgency.

SATURDAY, AUGUST 4TH. Pasta this evening earlier than usual, and a good deal quieter. It transpires that B., K. and Percy are all leaving for their new destinations at dawn. Honestly, you could hear the cheese being sprinkled, it was so quiet.

SUNDAY, AUGUST 5TH. A bejewelled Mediterranean morning. William, Coleridge and myself walk with our friends to Piazzale Roma. I feel it is the end of an era. We all know it is time to say goodbye. Yet somehow, somewhere, I felt sure that we were destined to meet again.

But this time it was not to be.

KEATS, John died Rome 1821: 'Our future was in his beginning.'

SHELLEY, Percy Bysshe, sailed into a storm on the Tyrehennian Sea, 1822: 'Yeah, yeah. For the 'undredth time. Izza rudder.'

BYRON, Lord George Gordon, lack of familiarity with the Greek rifle Missolonghi, 1824: 'His number was in Heaven's phonebook, but Hell could get him on the extension.'

COLERIDGE, Samuel Taylor, too much, Highgate, 1834: 'Amazing.'

WORDSWORTH, William, old age and flocks in the water, Meregrass 1850: 'Father Nature with a handle.'

WORDSWORTH, Dorothy, lack of Romantics, Meregrass, 1855: '

Sir Walter
and Jane

Inspired by the famous five, the early years of the nineteenth century turned into a really good Romantic Movement. Napoleon wanted the world; Turner fell in love with the sky; George III went mad; nothing in a skirt crossed the Alps without running into Casanova; and even Nelson said 'Kiss me Hardy.' Men were leaving home to write oodles of emotional poetry about geography; women had lovers at all hours of the night; and children realised their supreme ideological importance. It was a time when people of all ages, colours and creeds were being persuaded to extend, flourish and pass on quicker. It was a time of 'emotional polychromatic democracy', to quote a small American professor who visited us once.

Historically, it was the time of the Regent. Admittedly, the Regent only lasted for nine of the thirty seven years covered by this chapter, but you don't honestly want to hear about William IV do you? Of course, not. Right. So let's get excited about the spirit of the age, and make the whole thing seem like thirty seven. George III, George IV and William IV were indeed not dissimilar (see above).

Spiritually, they were linked by brandy and all hailed Waterloo as a return to normal drinking. Gin, according to Wellington, was also quite popular, but this being dry and made in London was best used for distilling patriotism. Brandy had more heroic uses – being generally decanted on a star-spangled chaise-longue to a background of green-striped wallpaper, to aid the digestion of eight-ton pheasants and the eventual consummation of the dinner guest who was – statistically – a leading actress. Exactly why Princes of Wales inevitably want to get their leg over actresses is a question outside the scope of this book. Anyway, let's accept for the time being that royalty, dandies and men in uniform were all as bad as one another, being raffish, full-bloodied, half-cut and giving it a rare old go down at the Brighton Pavilion. To put it briefly, things were pretty fast and loose.

And Prose, fully cultivated now, chimed in with the basic mood providing 2d. romances, erotic memoirs and horror stories. In fact, anything to keep the adrenalin going. Yet, from this turbulence on the printed page, two authors emerge whose books seem to have a peculiar fascination for uncles and aunts when they discover that their nephews and nieces have passed the age of twelve. By the time of one's twentieth birthday, Uncle Roland has usually discharged the complete works of Sir Walter Scott and reverted to sweaters, while Auntie Glynnis, unable to find any more Jane Austen, has retired into handkerchieves. However, back through the mists of time, let us go North first of all to Sir Walter Scott.

Sir Walter was undoubtedly one of the nicest chaps in Literature. He was a charming lawyer, fond of animals, living in a castle, happily married and very rich. But God did he love a story. Never have so many been married to so many, by just one. Furlong upon furlong of derring-do with fearless, honest, merry and hospitable Highlanders. In fact, Scott's bizarre concern for old Newts got so out of hand that I feel the Scottish National Tourist Board must hold some of the responsibility for this. Certainly, as a result of his labours, coachloads of tourists visited the Highlands, kilts were flogged by the ton, and a generation of innocent children finished up with names like Duncan and Jock. We can only hope that he got some commission out of it all. But then again you don't not give commission to Scottish lawyers, so I suppose that put an extra turret on the sunlounge.

Anyway, we ought really to be looking at Sir Walter as an historical novelist. So let's say at once that he was, in several respects, historical. Surely nobody has ever understood better the art of turning the printed page into the folding note:

Scott's law

Get yersel intae bizzniss wi'a printer.

Get yersel a share o'a bookshop.

Dinny till the reeder hooo yar. Draves 'em whiled.

Cha-up the reeder wi'preffusses an'hulp 'im oot
wi'appendixes. Times gi'im a wee rub wi'a glossary.

Naebody kens hoo rote yer books, review 'em yersel.
Y'cannae do better. Aye, y'can. Orn the magazine.

A free golf ball wi'ev'ry twenty five dust jackets
returned eh.

Collect £200 when y'pass Edinburgh.

On top of his acumen Scott had a compulsive wrist. It was a profitable combination of characteristics. By midday his study was more like a garage. Fit a few trappings here, mix a little padding there, adjust throttle on a speech in the corner, assemble syntax for after lunch.

Looking over his shoulder we see him at work on 'The Sword of Strathbane'. It might give us another perspective on the historical novelist. Or, to put it another way, why nobody I know seems to have read him, despite the fact that he existed.

'It was upon the evening of this memorable Sunday that our hero, or princeps, whom we have mentioned twice before, and will have occasion to mention again, found himself pacing with a stern step and a daunting echo the great flagstones of his vestibule lairdique. With his third gigantic step, a dimension of his tread which we have not mentioned before, our noble hero, the 18th Vulcan of Glennfiddich, took up a position upon the lefthand flank of the fireplace, in which he felt both security from sudden attack and winning warmth from the Promethean peat. At length, at the door of that worthy chamber, there came a stumbling and a knocking, at which aural provocation the Vulcan ripped his gimlet gaze from the red deer above the baldric, and turned to the offending door, issuing forth a mighty de facto Habeas Corpus.

The Bailie of Teachers wove into the room, a long chain from his foot having the captured English Captain Briscoe on the end of it. 'Bhithinn sgoil thig burp an tuathanach leabhar aig burp toilichte uaireadair adhearcan aran air a'bhord bottle of Glenn Campbell?' said that stalwart Bailie. 'Nae', returned the tremendous Vulcan to that unfortunate vassal. Captain Briscoe leapt into the breach with a salutation of great eagerness: 'I think there's a can of beer in my dufflebag.' And the aforementioned Bailie heaved a sigh of brave disgust, mingled with an immense relief, such that the hirsute orange sproutings from his eyebrows, nose and ears, stiffened and waved with renewed hope. 'Sassenach slop', roared the terrific Vulcan pulling forth a pocket watch the size of a cannon ball with a flick of the hand, 'They're awpen.' And at this point, our hero, the Bailie and Captain Briscoe betook themselves into the night, or tenebras, to continue their conversation at a convenient distance.

'Tis a lang wee at Inverary,
Wi' a sweetest dram I ken.'

Captain Briscoe knew that he was now being called upon to put up great resistance if he was not go give everything away to his persistent questioners. The King would expect a silence, in which his captors were unlikely to acquiesce. . . .'

This could never have been Jane speaking. Jane was a different kettle of fish. If any old Newts had tried to come wandering into her novels, she would have shown them the blotting paper at once. As for that sly young Captain Briscoe with beer in his dufflebag, he would never do. Not for young ladies of breeding at any rate.

Jane Austen was born at Steventon, the daughter of a Rector. She rose in her lifetime to become an acknowledged expert on the location of husband material in Southern England. Not a wide canvas perhaps, but Jane painted in great detail. She didn't actually provide names and addresses, but in a stream of such classic finishing novels as 'Marriage and Marriageability' and 'Cucumber Park', she did lay down a few golden rules about gentlemen whose prospects could be entertained.

By and large, they tended to hang round the Pump Room at Bath. So, Jane's first golden rule for a young girl snatching glances round the Pump Room is: only go out with clergymen, officers and landowners who look 10,000 a year, behave like robots, and know how to hold a tea cup. Your mother, with whose help you will agree upon a mutual selection, will then see to it that he is introduced to your needlework, sketching and accompanied singing. Don't at this stage judge him too quickly, lure him into a pathetic set-up, or elope with him. Just say that you hope he can afford to pay you a call, and accidentally drop a luggage label. He will start paying calls. You will gradually become wreathed in smiles at the sight of his carriage. And then one day, you will visit him. And then one day when you can't stop visiting each other, he'll pop the question. He will, of course, pop the right question or it's back to the Pump Room. Close your ears at once to any question preceded by agitated breathing and the word 'Look'. Gentlemen with honourable intentions issue a neat and relaxed 'Will you marry me?' And now a girl sorely needs prudent counsel. Is his bank manager on the phone? Does he have a modern kitchen? Will he have a vasectomy? How often does he expect a clean shirt? If you can answer 'yes' to these questions, reply: 'What a super idea.' Which brings us to Jane's greatest golden rule: marry for love, provided he's got enough money and doesn't like football. Remember the consternation in the Bennet household when it is discovered that Mr Bingley has played for Arsenal. And then it's just a matter of the Right Church and who to invite. This will need you to put your heads together, to find out who is being taken up, who is to be invited and then get snubbed, and who is to be invited and get a bit of cool treatment just as a warning. And then before you can say Volvo, Pony Club or Hunt Ball, it'll all be over and you've done it.

Before leaving Jane, the student must be alerted to her A-Level chestnuts. Why do her characters behave as they do? And what about that irony? However, we're a bit pushed for space, so I'd rather leave any detailed discussion of Jane Austen's heroines to the distaff side of the Faculty, most of whom have pretty severe systems for apportioning praise and blame amongst the dear young things. And when some of Jack's Amazonian girl-friends get going the pets really come in for a rough ride. Still, it is not known how many girls, foolish girls or sensible girls, went through the Jane Austen Marriage Brokers. But the famous irony is known. Try as they might, Jane wasn't having any.

Not to be worried by this little setback off the B3400 just west of Basingstoke, the Romantic Movement roared on.

In 1837 it came to an abrupt end. Few historians would quarrel with this judgement. Although I must admit that I sometimes get bouts of tetchiness with it, feeling that it's not normally possible to stop a man being passionate overnight. But then all my doubts disappear when I refresh myself with a picture of the Queen. The prospect of a miserable-looking dumpy little woman solemnly winding herself into acres of funereal linen and publicly declaring that she has no sense of humour and German relatives, must have filled the trains with returning husbands and knocked the bottom out of the drugs market. How could you be Romantic with that on the throne? Not, of course, that everyone was unhappy about the change of mood; barbers, tailors and milliners were delighted with all the new Victorian fathers. They hadn't had a break like this since the Civil War.

Voluminous Victorians

Use the word 'Victorian' as often as you like with train drivers, missionaries and philatelists. Say 'Victorian' to a statesman and you might catch a wistful glow. Mention 'Victorian' to an auctioneer or Poet Laureate and they'll whip out something for you and fondle it with joyous urbanity. Praise the Victorians to a Marxist and duck. There will be a negative response (−), temporarily unrelated to his dwelling in an up-and-coming Victorian terrace, which he will one day have to part with for a healthy profit (£++). Say what you like about the Victorians – and everyone seems quite happy with that arrangement – they shifted. And none more so than my great-grandfather Thomas Earnest Tweedcroft, a man who left Yorkshire without a pair of trousers, survived a hailstorm in the Pennines, and died owning more trouser factories in Lancashire than there were legs to go round. But say 'Victorian' to a literary man and things are reasonably straightforward.

and PhD men, a vast detritus of sermons, biographies, travel books, manuals and the endless novels of Mrs Horace Trinder, builds up in lumber rooms, secondhand bookshops and church fêtes. Not that it shouldn't. Read any two pages of it, and you either conceive an immunity to Literature or decide to have a go yourself.

But the good books, which is what we shall be dealing with here, were generally serialised in magazines, suitable for young ladies at their bedside, and welcomed upon publication by the Archbishop of Canterbury, a General, a Literary Lion, a society hostess, the Bishop of Oxford, one or two critics and the Queen. However, the people running and producing both Literature and Victorian England were not those around the throne. This was the age when Her Majesty's subjects in the middle rank strode into the limelight and earned for themselves all sorts of unpleasant reputations.

What they did to Drama hardly bears repeating. They called it Melodrama, whereas the Puritans at least had the decency to close the theatres altogether. But if you want a really good cry, witness the condition of poor old Will Shakespeare. A man called Bowdler took it upon himself to launder the plays for family use, with the result that the Victorians are the only people ever to have seen 'Coriolbottom' and 'King Smile'. And it's not every day you get a 'Twelfth Night' with Sir Toby Pardon. But then, some of them even went so far as to find the whole of Literature the work of the Devil. Visiting their dwellings, you might be lucky and find a novel lining the lid of a trunk in the attic but otherwise it was a few buns, a cup of tea and the pronouncements of the 47th Brethren of the Free Norwich Fathers. Others, to put it nicely, were too busy to read. Literature, to them, was the wellspring of idleness, bisexuality and theory in a lad who might otherwise be a good tradesman. So, no bookworming for him. As long as a lad knows that Prose is the stuff that goes to the end of the line, he can work out what Poetry is for himself.

Yet there were others in the middle strata, equally capable of reading, who positively turned to Poetry and

Prose. Why? Well frankly they were worried. Because all those sixth form debate subjects which make you sit down and think, begin now. Agnosticism or Sex? Man or Christian? Despot or Money? Class Structure or Censorship? Censorship and Religion or Money, Sex, War and Education? And when people opened a book they wanted shelter from this lot, or answers. After all, there were three times as many pubs per head of the population as there are now, ten thousand prostitutes in London, and group of men gathering evidence that the Bible was a load of cobblers. The Victorians found nothing funny in learning that the passage of the Israelites through the Red Sea in one night, advancing five abreast, would in fact have formed a column one hundred miles long – irrespective of baggage, sheep and cattle – and taken them well over a week. They found even less to laugh at when their descent was suddenly switched from Adam and Eve in Paradise, to some clever ape who'd made it out of the slime only to start rutting all over the place with all the other clever buggers.

And so it happened, quite understandably, that authors were now expected to take the Victorians out of themselves for a while, entertain them, or take them into their confidence and explain what Life was all about. We begin our examination with Poetry.

Poetry hit an initial snag of some magnitude. There weren't any poets. But just as no piano is complete without a cloth, the Victorians weren't going to accept this situation. Accordingly, Mrs Hemans and Martin Tupper became best sellers, the successors to Straightspeare, given at weddings, 21st birthdays and confirmations, and nearly knighted. Our essential difficulty in appreciating this is that nobody has ever heard of them. Alfred Lord Tennyson, however, is different. We've all heard of him, and probably eaten some of his rock at Freshwater Bay. And he was made a Lord. Although for years I thought that was his middle name. Still, when someone insists on going around underneath a sombrero with a cloak and stick there must be somewhere in the back of his mind either an arrowed jersey or a bit of ermine. And Tennyson, having been to a Grammar School, certainly wasn't going to put up a fight if the big rodent fur came along. He hadn't bought a house in the Isle of Wight, fifteen miles south west of the Queen, just to be blown about all over the downs.

Tennyson became an oracle. People took to writing in their diaries what they were doing, or where they were going to when a new Tennyson came out. But Alfred, tall, elegant, a bit of a chain smoker, gave them a lovely feeling. Six hundred lemmings go belting up the wrong alley and it's:

> 'Half a league, half a league,
> Half a league onward.'

The vexed question of women hits the headlines, and Alfred steps in:

> 'Woman is not undevelopt man
> But diverse;. . .'

Religion comes under attack and there's nearly a public holiday when it's learnt that Alfred 'faintly trusted the larger hope'. Still they might have known what to expect when he won his prize medal at Cambridge with 'Timbuctoo'. But what did they care really? You could have some lovely quasi-sexual afternoons lolling on the sunny bank of a quiet river with Alfred. He understood rhythm. And he wasn't afraid to borrow from all ages. One moment its geology, the next moment it's Camelot. But never so optimistic that the spell breaks. Lots of tears and tender roses, like a sweet ache. About the only time the spell did break was when Alfred had one of his attacks of reading aloud. There was no knowing when this would happen, but a bottle of port was a good start. Sometimes not even that would be necessary, as the fishermen of Freshwater Bay occasionally discovered. Alfred just got into the boat.

Contrary to popular belief, Browning was not undevelopt Tennyson, but diverse. In fact, so diverse that he is at times a little dark in meaning. Alas, 'Sordello' his first ben trovato masterpiece, being a poetic acrostic of selected newspaper headlines, and telling the story of a diminutive twelfth-century, deaf Italian troubadour's passionate fight to re-organise the chaos of local government as he found it under the Bologna of the Wristini, left ninety percent of his readers at the title. When this was followed by 'Bells and Pomegranates' the publishers asked Browning to consider seriously whether he thought a bookshop his best outlet, covering themselves by sending pilot copies to green grocers and off-licences. To be fair, Browning was enigmatically explicit about the fact that he didn't know what his poetry meant. You only have to look at a passage full of dashes and question marks to see that he doesn't know what's going on any more. When this happens you should consult a Browning Society who, at 20p to cover the cake, will lovingly bend you through the difficult patches, and see intellectual landmines in what you thought were the easy bits. Doubt that anything so innocuous as 'The Ring of the Book' is going to be anything less than the telephone directory backwards, as seen by the female members of a Sicilian funeral cortège.

So did Browning actually have a message for the Victorians? Something that perhaps wouldn't need a team of German philosophers on amphetamines? Well, yes he did. But the essential point is that it was more in his body than in his mind. Browning set a trend for keeping fit. Which is the least anyone can do when they're considering how to get an invalid and her dog down a drainpipe in Wimpole Street. Moreover, it's got to be done quietly and the invalid is, unfortunately, a poetess. But this wasn't going to stand in Browning's way. Browning had translated two plays about Hercules, and regularly slept in a jock strap. He wasn't going to give in. In letter after letter, he sent her travel brochures, suntan cream, goggles, flippers, beach balls, things about the Renaissance and, of course, details of the plan. But there was always something going wrong. Elizabeth liked Pisa, but the dog had bitten him; she was ill; someone had nicked Flush; the old man smelt a rat; he'd pulled a muscle in training. But a little jogging to loosen the hamstrings and a long weekend ogling gutters, and Browning felt fit for the drainpipe. The results are legendary in the history of English Literature, which admittedly isn't very tough opposition, though Dryden might have run him close. Browning, by all accounts, did well.

Later in life, through the character of Fra Umberto Houdini, a fourteenth-century Neopolitan fireman, Browning spills out those airborne moments in Wimpole Street:

Why, the only canine I construe is *Woof* –
So, have it all out! Zooks, there's for you! *Woof!*
Now! Down the knotted sheet! *Advance, you Soul!*
Fit to infinity your finite part!
What? Not adorn our Medusan cameo?
I'll open you on a three-part tryptych.
(*Oh, to be in Rome rather than up here!*)

141

Bah, my love; dangling my Gordian beauty?
Hang on! There's no market for street mosaics.
What cheek had I to say that then, *eh? Eh?* –
E'en priests know the Whole we achieve by Parts.
But I was younger afore, and much higher
To God than I am now to your fingers,
Stretch, my Bah! And bend! Remember, my love? –
We get on fast to see the bricks beneath.
Still, but young once and that's all behind us –
Ouf! Go on, it's your turn to get the tea,
Leave me dream of Heaven and Earth and Sheets,
The Serpentine in Hyde Park? And the like.
Zooks, the only canine he construed was *Woof!*

Possibly as a result of Browning leaping around encouraging fitness and happy marriages a group of people with double-barrelled names decided to form a club. Their names don't actually provide much of a clue as to why they did get together. The motive was apparently the worship of anything Pre-Raphaelite, which could have given disturbingly wide carte blanche for any lonely Victorian who wished to have a pretext for surrounding himself with a whole crop of new mates. But there was one distinguishing feature of the new Pre-Raphaelite Brotherhood: not one of their double-barrelled names had a hyphen. Otherwise Holman Hunt sounds like a merchant banker, Madox Brown like a JP who invented cough medicine, Everett Millais like an aristocratic student of bird seed, while Burne Jones was probably an Ear, Nose and Throat specialist who played squash once a week. Dante Gabriel Rossetti sounds a little more arty, but he was an Italian with both feet in the air – not strong on definitions. Not that they didn't have great fun trying to define the movement. God knows, they did – noisily rushing up and down stairs, breaking into rooms and impatiently pulling off door bells if they felt something of the way forward had occurred to them. But most of the time it was just a question of lassooing passive women who looked like Raphael's auntie at thirteen and having Gothic relationships with intensely close friends. Basically then the Pre-Raphaelite movement was a sort of Oxford and Chelsea thing which you either understood, or got a job.

But for those who did more or less understand, Mecca was No. 16 Cheyne Walk. Here Rossetti and friends were occupying a house, and achieving wonders of ambidexterity as painter-poets. Although, whichever hand held the paint brush was definitely the stronger one. You could write some Pre-Raphaelite poetry yourself if you wanted to. Just look at one of their paintings, light a joss stick, have a glass of very cold water, and eke out some precise and sensuous details about the nostalgic and titillatingly unobtainable delights of the maiden in the picture. However, don't then do what Rossetti did with his poems. So upset was he by the death of his wife, that he buried his poetry with her. So upset was he by his wife's death, he didn't feel like writing any more poems. So upset was he by not being able to write any new poetry, he did the only thing possible and dug up the wife – drenching the poems in disinfectant and publishing them. Rossetti later fell in love with William Morris's wife, who, being more than a little anxious to outlive him, did more exercises and read more Browning than anyone else in the whole century.

The Pre-Raphaelite way of life was somewhat more irregular than its artistic mood. They could be rather unreliable house guests. Rossetti went to stay at someone's house while they were away, got dissatisfied with the architecture, knocked a wall down, removed the kitchen etc etc, decided it was all wrong, blew the whole lot up and left a note. Mind you, that was a let-off compared to actually staying with Rossetti. To ease the general ebb and flow of No. 16, Gabriel had given over the garden, and strategic areas in the house to a Brahmin bull, zebras, gazelles, racoons, peacocks, kangaroos, parrots, wombats, marmots, owls, squirrels, rabbits, wolfhounds, porcupines, mice and an elephant trained to clean the windows. Cadogan leases have been tightened up a fair bit since Rossetti. Which is hardly surprising when a missing armadillo returns through the floor of a neighbour's kitchen; when Rossetti regularly forgets to feed them for a month, whereby they feel compelled to eat each other, each other usually disputing this view in a manner fit to be audible somewhere in Kent; and then, at last, when you go round to complain, a fucking wombat eats your hat.

The loud barrage of weird grunts, strange cries and awful smells coming from No. 16 was not ameliorated by the presence of an unidentified flying object called Swinburne. You nearly whistle saying the name. And you'd certainly whistle if you ever saw him. He had the most famous hair in English Literature: an inverted orange fan, billowing downwards like a spaniel storing food in its ears. Not washed, it tended to straggle. And then he'd scream the house down if you called him 'Carrots'. However, a Swinburne scream is not quite what it might appear at first sight. Although not awfully good at restraint, Algy was very fond of being restrained – in fact tied up and hit with whips, rubber hammers etc. Eton was paradise for him, a paradise he never thought he'd regain till he found porcupines in the garden. There was just one little hitch though. Rossetti also used them, for combing his hair, which to Swinburne's way of thinking was a sacrilegious waste of a good porcupine, and led to frequent running battles in the corridors, during which priceless examples of blue bone china went drastically astray. In the end Rossetti bought a comb. Fighting with Algy, he discovered was expensive and ultimately useless. He loved it if he lost, and didn't mind winning either 'cos he'd got his porcupine back.

But the main trouble about flat-sharing with Swinburne was not really the long ritual of sobering him up for dinner, and requesting that he wear some clothes for this event, but more that if he hadn't said anything brilliant by nine o'clock he was under guarantee to say something diabolical before ten o'clock. And then your only hope was that he might *eschewinglissh'n'sebbin' Fressh* whereupon you could probably get away with him.

Of course, when Algy had one of his own thrashes

things were a bit different. Very different. A room full of undergraduate disciples, plenty of wine and equipment, with Algy, supreme on a table, declaiming poetry. The heady rhythms, the shocking content; the blasphemy, the pain, the sea; and Algy's voice rising, piercing, rolling, skewering several octaves above the ensuing mêleé. A Swinburne party came but once a week, to allow time for repairs. Algy usually got them all going with his 'Hymn to Nemesis'.

Hymn to Nemesis

O Mother,
Which art aflame with blame,
Hallowed be thy Nemesis!
Thy Devildom come
To drench us in shame,
Shallow be my genesis!
O, but with thy will, we will be done
One by one by one by one
With throngs of thongs
Till legs be leaven,
And give us this night bloody Heaven
And lead us not into cessation,
Sliver us into weevils,
For thine's the power of expiation
Ours the joy of evils.

Algy was really too much of a raver for the Victorians. This was NOT their idea of having a few friends round. And when Algy made a kamikaze attempt to pull his socks up – placing himself under house arrest with a teetotaller in Putney – who confiscated an emergency supply of hedgehogs – Purity's vanguard was not appeased. There were about Mr Swinburne, said the Victorians, straightening their backs and pushing their chests out, irregularities. And Mr Rossetti, for that matter, could do far worse than to acquaint himself with the long distance capacities of a steamship. If the Pre-Raphaelites were not roundly condemned for being weird and sexy, then Sir, the morality of Art would soon take over. And, where, pray, would we be then?

Painter-poets, if left unchecked, were the thin end of the ungodly wedge. Still, they were also a colourful mist over Victorian coketowns; and a splash of pure joy compared to pictures of Highland cattle before a thunderstorm, or portraits of Queen Victoria letting you know what it's like to spend half your life pregnant when you're trying to run an Empire.

But it wasn't quite all over for Poetry yet. There were still a few more pages up its sleeve. There was, for example, 'The Rubaiyat of Omar Khayyam' by Edward Fitzgerald. Another shocker. Wine is mentioned. There was also the Victorian speciality of light verse, tripping from the pens of gentlemanly semi-pros by the ton and generally measured out in secondhand bookshops by the yard. Meanwhile, answers of integrity to the problems of Victorian life had virtually disappeared from the bardic page. However, Matthew Arnold intended to make up for all that.

It was at Rugby School, where his father, Dr Thomas Arnold, was, to say the least, in charge, that early signals were first picked up of an extraordinarily spacious and delicate technology between the ears of Arnold minor. As a result of this find, and notwithstanding the fact that Rugby had been the first school in the land to go Latin on the pitch, Matthew was only allowed to play in the easier fixtures – provided, that is, he wore a reliable scrum cap and shunned any scenes of escalating violence.

Matthew was parachuted into Oxford as soon as possible. His mission: to locate the wavelength of Truth through twiddling the knobs of Poetry, and then turn up the volume. Late Victorian England hung in the balance. And it was here and now, in the city of dreaming spires, that Arnold minor, through long walks and cold baths, attempted to convert his body into one hundred percent pure spirit. Interference lessened. His steps lightened. His thoughts turned to buying a pen. He put flowers in his room. He punted down the Isis. He thought for days on end. And then bought a pen. The long silence was close to breaking point:

'Who prop, thou ask'st, in these bad days, my mind?'

146

asked Matthew, in a line of poetry worthy of the later Beethoven. But he was on the right lines. He'd inherited from his old man the mantle of leading the world out of trouble through exposure to himself at the earliest possibility. The only trouble at the moment was that he didn't know the answer to the question. He went to France for a think.

Back in England, Matthew was still stumped. Yet aware with increasing poignance that only he could answer this question. He was beginning to move around

like a hearse. Oxford again. Filled his room. Even more flowers. A few statues. Threw open all the windows. And then suddenly it came to him in a flash: Sweetness and Light. Of course. Anyone who didn't understand that obviously hadn't spent fifteen years thinking about it. But wait. It was a conclusion of such enormity that poetry probably couldn't carry it. Matthew would have to start writing prose and go round the schools.

Periodically, Matthew returned to the Oxford he loved. Walking the hills picking daisies, he'd get very depressed that nobody seemed to be taking any notice of his message, and started pulling dandelions to bits. It wasn't as if he hadn't tried. He'd told the English they were basically moronic, and given them a new class system. Should have been an irresistible combination.

The fact that it wasn't, worried Matthew perhaps a teeny bit more than it should have done. After all, his vision of English football crowds reconsidering Heine and Spinoza while the staff of British Rail joust in elegant paradox with bingo hall queues over the later Schopenhauer, was now just one of many answers to the ever-popular 'condition of England' question. Competition for the public ear was most eager. And with Poetry now more or less completely gaga, sages were pouring into Speaker's Corner faster than the orange boxes could be shifted there.

Over this welter of opinion towered the two Great Sages. Firstly, a man who would stand no blasted nonsense. Thomas Carlyle. Carlyle's father, a stone mason of essential goodness, forbade him toys and wanted him to be a bishop. Carlyle responded by setting himself up in secular headquarters at Cheyne Row, Chelsea, having thoroughly roamed the moors of Dumfriesshire as one does in time of mental depression, preparing for this new address. By now the student might have gathered that Carlyle was not an optimist. The student has gathered correctly. Carlyle was famous for great bellows of Woe. He is the Victorian doom-watcher sans pareil, sans nuclear shelter, sans everything. Never a silver lining without a cloud! A pipe bursts, and he goes rushing through the house looking for the Bible; the fire smokes, and it must be an earthquake. But the thing about Carlyle was that if he got into a state, he put everyone into a state. Nothing the wife didn't know about this of course. But it was her choice. He started sending books to her, which is how women who want to marry literary geniuses expect to be chatted up.

The process didn't last long. They soon started writing letters to each other for posterity's sake; she even ended up signing 'Yours Faithfully'. That was in the letters. In real life, the china closest was like the one round the corner in Cheyne Walk – more a source of ammunition than decorative effect.

Still, as someone at the time commented, in marrying each other they at least made only two people unhappy. Carlyle, on the other hand, could make everyone unhappy. You never knew where you were with a sage: he might smoke his pipe all evening and say nothing or talk non-stop till the Ovaltine. And when he was writing, he really 'had' a book. Everything was wrong, there wasn't a bit of bad news he couldn't trump, and the only chance of a two-way conversation was when he was shaving. In fact, the prize for the Stickiest Moment in Literature goes to J.S. Mill when he has to tell Carlyle what happened to the first volume of 'The French Revolution'. Mill hadn't even got round to reading the manuscript before his servant lit the fire with it. And if Mill hadn't been a philosopher that's probably what Carlyle would have done with him. However, although we don't yet light fires with Carlyle, we don't perhaps turn to him with quite the same urgency. For some reason he never discovered the short sentence, which is unfortunate, as a mature Sherpa is needed for the longer ones. Apart from this setback, there's also Carlyle's engaging belief that one could blast off at the universe from a lonely, personal rock and frighten it into surrendering its mysteries by sheer force of rhetoric. His version of 'Jesus wept' from 'Bismarck Benedictus' is only one piece of lava from the volcano:

'*Jesus;* – nay, Reader, my brother properly speaking, my
hero, indispensablest Nazarene Mahomet on the planet Earth,
eight parts Water were we not immethodic quack-heads –!– let
us co-öperate; show a man a tuppenny candle and he will have
Light! – all true illumination is Fire! – yet the Great Galilean
cheek has moisture?! – whitherward? – why should the tear
prove logically that it ought to flow as the Waters of Heaven,
Earth, Hell, London ever, we say, will do?–;–!– or was it mere
sweat of the brow through vigiliance of good victual? – no-
whither: there is falsity in this problem; forget that, thou has
forgotten all; tears, they were, such as even mighty Behemoth
could tell you of; tears, they were, such as, among men, the
Captain-General of Handkerchieves alone could staunch, trus-
ting in God and keeping his linen dry, drier than Sahara still
– for One as Three – yea, God – has; – *wept.*

John Ruskin, too, could pull out something pretty long,

hot and purple when it came to sentences. In one paragraph, he could give you more neckwork than the central
court in Wimbledon in an afternoon. But come rain or
shine, you'd be lucky to get a definite result out of him.
It wasn't that he didn't finish. It was more that his ideas
seemed to change with the moon – and then proceed
with all the fertility of a well-struck shot on a pinball
table. He bumps into 'x' and explodes; brushes with 'y'
and lights up; bounces back into 'x' for the second time
and changes his mind; boings into 'y' and reproduces a
facsimile explosion of his first contact with 'x'. Art criticism seemed the natural place for him to begin.

Ruskin zoomed straight off into the subject. Free from
all the usual constraints, impatient of contradiction, he
covered anything from frescoes to garden tools. Some of
his heaviest collisions were with Architecture. Any
society that did not construct itself upon Gothic princi-
ples was, he said, in danger. In danger of spiritual rot,
economic collapse, tidals waves of immorality and
normal tidal waves. We should therefore at the earliest
opportunity model our buildings upon those of C15th
Venice. And the Victorians being Victorians, and loving
nothing better than a good warning, carried out Ruskin's
advice at existentially sensitive areas like public lavato-
ries, town halls and railways. And now you can't enjoy
a pint in South London without having some saving
cusped arch peering into your glass, or some foliated
capital casting benediction on your bird.

Fortunately when Brother John came to bless political
economy his views did not receive immediate implement-
ation. Happy workers' souls were to be the basis of the
economy. Shop stewards were to be replaced by gurus.
It was all just a case of up at dawn, wipe the dew
off the anvil, prayers and breakfast, whistle while you
hammer till twilight, and then sing your heart out
reblacking the anvil for the morrow. Ruskin of course
wasn't able to talk to any medieval craftsmen; but he
was able to write 'Letters to the Workmen and Labourers
of Great Britain'. Whether or not this amounted to
communication remains to be seen:

Letter XCVI

Friends,

As I am sitting here correcting this sheet, and beside me lies an address to the working men of Burnley's Downright Unco-operative Society, under my window is a man with a cart and a horse of no great incentive. So will you be good enough to further your education and attend to what I have to say? By all means eat your sandwiches when reading this, I usually have a lump of fruit cake and a pot of Greek tea.

Now, by your leave, returning to our horse for a moment. It should be of especial interest to us to observe how unquickly this civic quadruped is moving. Why doesn't he go faster you ask? Is he too old? Is he soon for the knacker's yard, and thence, at huge profit to someone, onto your dinner plates? Does his owner – for that is what he is, until such time as we can lease horses, my friends – never think to stretch a quantity of sugar across his blinkers? For at that time when Pegasus was alive, it was half a pound of caster sugar to the Acropolis or Shank's pony, Perseus! No, my friends, it is of vital importance for you to realise that the answer to this whole situation lies underneath. Yes, my friends, I am talking now of the roads. Obliged by capitalism though you are to be our representatives in this sphere, I know this much for your benefit, if I know anything: quadrupeds will never accelerate, nor one 'owner' be able to share his raised standard of living with you, nor on one day of the week will you arrive on your doorsteps from work cleaner and sweeter smelling – until such time as we have wooden roads.

Paths of oak, my friends, paths of oak. Is that not the very thing I am telling you? Promise me 'Highways of oak are our roads' will be your meditation for a week. Are they not easier to put down? May we not than have more and lighter vehicles travelling faster? All, I say, will be silence compared to iron over cobbles. And do not forget that we should build little trap doors for moles, so that Nature can return to our roads. Respecting the position of moles have no fears of elongated carnage. They will soon develop an inbuilt Darwinian sense of timing about when to pop up.

As things have gone hitherto, who, I can hear you ask, will pay you to construct these roads? Not the moles, assuredly; they will be waiting down below. Yourselves, friend, is the answer to this one. And now note this that follows. Leave this capitalistic tarmac; live together; work together. I will even give you a name: The Knights of the Heart of Troy. It may be that you start in an outlying area, free from soot, dust and filth, then friends, work towards the centre of a town and sell your road to the Government. Think on it labores mes; next month I intend to deal with stone cutlery.

And so believe me,
Faithfully yours,
JOHN RUSKIN

The Victorians weren't very happy with John about this. Nor did they appreciate William Morris, poet, chippy and lefty, when he started swinging a socialist cross in the air. Though they might be happier with Brother William's descendants today, most of whom seem to be doing off-beat things for up-market minorities, from small workshops with gilded waiting lists – if, that is, you want a not inexpensive little clock out of wire and cork, or a gentleman's afternoon smoking pipe in Cornish tin, pre-heated to 49.5 degrees Centigrade and personalised in luminous yoghurt. This last ingredient, handed down through the centuries is made from Real Goats, and is EXTRA + VAT + Anything Else I Can Think Of, at 20 Guineas.

Sages and poets came and went. But nobody opened Victorian eyes wider and longer than the Great Novelists. All the classes and regions of England flowered across the page, almost as if teams of publishers had worked out in advance who would cover whom in which area. Anyhow, at last, we can relax and enjoy them and their stories, which ambled much like our own lives, and yet because penned by kindly and sharp-eyed uncles or intelligent ladies from the country, were just as able to give our consciences a little joggle too. Make yourself cosy reader, snap into a bar of chocolate, put the kettle on, stoke the fire, sling the cat out, and pass instructions to the dog to bring your slippers.

We go by stage-coach first of all to Haworth, pulling up at the Rectory door in order to meet the Brontës – Charlotte, Emily, Anne, father Patrick and exploding

153

brother Burpwell. Burpwell, deeply upset about having three very quiet sisters in the middle of the Yorkshire moors, had long since gone to the bottle and taken to bizarre late-night performances on the local church organ – which only served to give Haworth a spurious Muslim flavour and plethoric outbursts of atheism. Still, the Reverend Patrick Brontë wasn't going to over-react. His main concern was to sit in the kitchen and wonder why Brontë had two little dots at the end. He could see how they suited the girls and Burpwell, but were his own perhaps originally some small, discreet token of celestial approval which dust and parish records had unfairly reduced to this hovering moth-eaten dash? Or was there a good pedigree in mystical horizontal colons? Lord, it was a tough nut. And, frankly, he didn't have the crackers.

Nor, alas, did he get much further when it came to understanding his daughters. Quite what Emily was on he never discovered. But then all three of them fair throbbed with mystery. Every quarter of an hour the Rectory clock chimed into silence without a dicky bird from the girls. Because, basically, each was rigid with fantasies of haunting Titanic men in earth-shattering thunderstorms, fleeing through vast, deserted mansions wrapped in enigma and only an old nightie, crimes of hurricane passion and orgasms of wondrous, exhausting reconciliation. But not a bleep. You could hear the dust gathering.

At times, of course, it was only natural that the strain would tell, that tensions would release themselves. One day, for example, towards tea-time when Emily for no apparent reason smashes Charlotte over the head with a stepping stone. This was the beginning of 'Wuthering Heights'. And the end of Charlotte's appearances at tea-time for a while. Not that Charlotte herself had been a model daughter during 'Jane Eyre'. Twice in one week the Rectory had experienced sudden gains in heat. All in all, 3 a.m. was about the best time to catch the Brontës.

3 a.m. was a bit early to meet Trollope. He usually started writing at 5.30 a.m. until three thousand words

had been completed by 8.30 a.m., after a few years of which he decided it was about time to invent post-boxes.

Trollope, initially treated with caution by the Victorian public until they found out that he was an expert on vicars, is one of the few authors whose literary worth can be weighed easily. TI = PB4 is the usual way of representing this, whereby one year of Trollope's output would fill four post-boxes. Needless to say, pictures of Scott festooned his study. But one new facet now twinkled for the library author of the bookshelf classic: reader participation. Trollope only saw the early days of reader participation – just a few scattered demos and rallies, early-morning poster bearers filing past his window with 'Barchester Against Clericism', 'Up the Dean', 'No Motorway Through Barchester', 'Trollope for God', 'The Warden is Great' etc. Not until Dickens were they actually writing the books. Yet none of this, for a moment, must detract from Trollope's lifelong study of Parsonus Anglicus Erratus.

Meanwhile, back in central London, William Makepeace Thackeray was making it very uncomfortable for snobs. What was he making uncomfortable? Well, everything, my dear. One simply couldn't go anywhere without bumping into Mr Thackeray, and his note-pad.

One dare not give a party without him; and one was terrified to give one with him. Only recently one was hearing distressing reports from Charterhouse Open Day of hastily departing carriages crushing strawberries into the lawn as word passed of Mr Thackeray's advance across the games field. And do you remember the adverse publicity which followed poor Lady Cutglance's party when Mr Thackeray had actually measured his measure, and examined the quality of the chalk in the billiard room? Well, I can tell you, my dear, we did. Our grandfather used to make the chalk. But that's strictly between you and I of course. I shall deny it strongly if challenged by Mr Thackeray. Oh I do wish he'd leave us alone. I swear we'd be on the first page if he wrote a book about Cathay. Mr Thackeray would then no doubt proceed to discover some connection between himself and the Ming Dynasty. Still, he is with us. And I suppose it does put one's guests on their best behaviour if he is there. But I do wish they wouldn't keep grovelling to him so. They positively turn one's soirée into a sorting office, so desperate are most of them to try and appease the old sherbert lemon. By the way, Edwin gave him a polo stick and it seems to have gone down quite well.

While quite a lot of people were partial to Mr Thackeray, lots more people were wildly in love with Charlie

Dickens. Nurtured by his parents on jellied eels in the hope that one day he would become a chimney sweep, Charlie Dickens threw it all away and became a journalist. In fact the most popular journalist in the entire history of the whole world. Stories and characters were air and water to Charlie Dickens. They were also bread and butter, as Charlie knew only too well at the end of every month, diving into his seat, furiously scanning which characters were going well, who to drop, and generally what to write next. Outside the public waited anxiously. Dickens Day was vital to the nation's mood. A good instalment was greeted with scenes reminiscent of a war and a football match being over at the same time. First editions changed hands at hilarious prices. Laughter ran amok.

Yet there were times when Charlie had to dispose of characters and occasion much grief. Few were the households that didn't have their tears phialed. Along any shelf you'd see the familiar rows of glass tubes with their damp legends. . .Little Nell, December '41. . .Paul Dombey, Easter '48. . .Bill Sikes's Dog. . .till the watery eye came to rest on the large sealed bucket at the end proclaiming Charlie, June 1870. Of no other author could it be said that childhood, Christmas, the fireside, a good laugh and a good cry would be incomplete without him. The reader is requested to observe a two minute break.

George Eliot and Thomas Hardy were quite different. You wouldn't want their stuff around on a festive occasion – unless perhaps if Jeremiah threw an At Home on Good Friday, and the drink ran out before 8.30. Anyhow, be that as it may, we shall now have to examine the effect upon the countryside of the modern novel.

The Great Rural Depression in late nineteenth century England is often wildly attributed to things like urban development, the new technology etc. etc. whereas in fact the main cause was Thomas Hardy. One simply can't explain away huge troughs of yokels moping in the doldrums by reference to the expansion of Dorchester, the advent of the remote-controlled plough or the cost-ineffectiveness of the plastic horseshoe. Even without the microclod, this dark chapter in rustic affairs must lay squarely on the desks of Thomas and George. A meeting with Mr Hardy is inevitable.

Thomas Hardy was an architect who decided that writing novels was a good way of depressing people. And, like most architects, built his own extraordinarily ugly house to provide an initial source of depression for anyone resilient enough to want to visit him. It took a public outcry after 'Jude in The Manure' to convince Hardy that he really was the most most depressing man in England. At this satisfactory point in his career, Hardy gave up novels and doomed off into poetry. Some of his brighter moments, though, twinkle through dimly in the extremely early works, e.g. 'Far From Merrie England':

Dan Barchurch returns home to Flintpuddle having lost his life's savings and an arm in the market at Wurzelock, only to find that his house has been struck by lightning, his wife's brains knocked out by a chimney pot and his only son mangled in a cider press on his first birthday. Dan begins to suspect that Fate is against him, experiencing a strange paralysis of will during which he takes to drink until finally forced, through starvation, to accept the post of pig-trusser on light duties up at Oxtrench Farm – run by the weak-willed Eustace Oxtrench, whose headstrong wife Horatia is widely hated in the village for not having any bad luck to speak of. Dan falls in love with Horatia, who finds his attentions revolting and allows herself to be seduced by a visiting Army Captain to spite Dan, and incidentally have a good time.

In a fit of hopelessness Dan marries Mop, a redundant twine-spinner from Dethridge, who imagines that he is a man of means. Dan alters his way enough to get Mop pregnant, realises what he's done, and suffers a period of domestic procrastination.

However, presented with a son, Dan finds that his feelings for the dependable Mop deepen into love. Whilst, on the farm, Eustace Oxtrench rewards his work with promotion.

Meanwhile in the village Gideon Trill, lanky tenor fiddle in the church choir, has been boasting of an inheritance, and of his intention to become music teacher extraordinary at Oxtrench Farm. One night at The Three Ravens, he lets slip of a lucky find at Wurzelock, though when confronted by Dan, denies the appearance of the circumstances. So when Dan hears that Oxtrench suspects his wife of having an affair, he resolves to discredit Trill by leaving a bonnet and plectrum in a haystack. Oxtrench is led to them, and leaves Dan the farm in his will, before bursting into the music room and leaving Gideon Trill with the definitive interpretation of a fiddle.

Eustace Oxtrench is carted off to jail, where he dies. Horatia goes off in pursuit of Captain Hastings, and is not heard of for years. Dan and Mop prosper on the farm, lose a few of their children and then begin to quarrel more often. It is during one of these rows that Dan confesses his trickery of Gideon Trill, something which Mop cannot live with. Gradually, guilt gives way to madness and Mop sets fire to herself. Full of remorse Dan works on.

Till one day a letter arrives from Horatia. She is returning, has proof of Trill's crime, whilst also admitting that he was for a short time her lover. After much soul-searching, Dan agrees to meet her. Waiting at the coach stop, he is suddenly overwhelmed by the surge of his buried love for Horatia and starts running to intercept her at a stop further up the line. He has not gone one mile before a frantic leap to avoid a nest of adders lands him in a wodge of Dorset quicksand, where the Wheel of Fate intervenes for the last time in the lives of Dan Barchurch and Horatia Oxtrench.

George Eliot's tampering with the yokel psyche took a slightly different course, as one might expect from a woman called George. Her role in the Great Rural Depression was to blow the bumpkin mind with a staggering number of moral choices. Indeed, it's a tribute to her philosophical mind that she chose for many years to live with someone also called George. However, far from encouraging a spate of bucolic transvestites, George was very stern about love – as she was, basically, about everything. To read George, the smallest twists and turns of living in the Midland Counties were like having breakfast with Mensa on a twenty-four hour basis. From socks on to teeth out, every minute of every day was imbued with reflection and decision.

'This is the story of Judas Harness, until the fifth minute after he came down Lunton High Street in the fourth-and-sixtieth of his life. . .Unsteadiness of gait can be a ground of surprise only to those who are unacquainted with that mode of locomotion which has gone on in the greater part of the geriatric community in our towns and villages, since time unrelenting. . .Though, as with many honest and fervent men, elegance of transport had not on many occasions occupied the superior channels of his divining. . .So when Judas Harness said "Yer 'andkerchuff", pointing solemnly all the while to the ground before him with the air of a man who grudgingly comprehended his physical metamorphosis, yet still retained the faculties of acute eyesight and ingratiating willingness to assist, it was in one respect a defeat that he could no longer oblige by precipitate action, and a triumph in the other that he had actually wanted to see it and had not summoned a convenient myopia. . .A little incident happened which shows this aspect further. . .'

George desperately wanted the Victorians to be on the ball. Oscar Fingall O'Flahertie Wills Wilde wasn't too fussed whether they even found the pitch.

On all the right occasions, he charmingly gave them all the wrong advice. With a tongue faster than the ear Oscar could twinkle sound advice into luminous nonsense and vice versa back again before the average Victorian had lodged his monocle and come to a full realisation of the fact that it was Monday. The Victorians never caught up with Oscar but they did eventually, as it were, halt in his wake. A magician of preposterous lucidity, Oscar would keep singing on about Beauty which the Victorians knew nothing about, except that it was British. Or at least they'd always thought it was. But then a Beauty expert who collected sheaves of peacock fans, velvet egg warmers, bone china and put a bold face on 'the love that dare not loosen its trousers' was not quite the sort of chap they had in mind for running the Empire. In fact he was more the sort of chap who'd go down better in Reading Gaol.

On the grounds that tomorrow's leaders might be being scuppered in our boarding schools through over exposure to Beauty and associated Hellenic hijinks, Oscar was incarcerated. But for those Victorians who couldn't find their way out of a paper bag without Burke's Peerage and the Bible the thought of Oscar breaking up proverbs down at Her Majesty's was not sufficiently cathartic. A brisk trade in Oscar effigies kept their indignation topped up.

Although awfully upset with Oscar, the Victorians hadn't honestly had an easy century. They'd had all the Guidance; but plenty of shocks too. And, as we've seen, some of them from literary men. If Charlie hadn't made them laugh and Tennyson soothed their pulses, several other men of the pen might have trodden the flagstones for their different reasons and mentioning no names, Rossetti and Hardy. In final defence of the Victorians one should perhaps add that having to umpire the Romantics at one end of their era and stop the world blowing itself up at the other end, they were badly sandwiched. Wouldn't anyone want to work hard and be a bit defensive? I expect that at midnight on December 31st 1899 when nineteenth century literature came to an end, the Victorians too breathed a sigh of relief.

On Your Marx, Get Set, Freud

Scholars have long been aware that as Literature mounts up more and more people will be writing about less and less, until one arrives at some hypothetical point in the future at which Literature and Silence will break even. What to do then is a constant source of panic at Pidgin College. Presumably start all over again with Ceefax poems and video pens. However, on the morning of January 1st 1900 that daunting point of eventual silence must have seemed much closer, as twentieth century literature shortened its sentences, streamlined its paragraphs and raced away off the starting blocks.

So why all the hurry? Well the main reason was an Oedipal desire to duff the Victorians for living in England and breathing. They could also be duffed for not having had a revolution or providing suitable toilet training. What a wonderful time it was going to be for talking and telling, for fathers and sons to have a swing at one another.

Behind all this were two stirrers, Marx and Freud. They are nowadays widely acknowledged as advance destabilising tools of Axis foreign policy, though in the extravagances of later German foreign policy this is sometimes overlooked. The stage was all set for Drama to return to our shores.

Drama, after resting between centuries, re-awoke to find itself in a fog of Nordic gloom and bearded playwrights, known simply as the New Drama. And indeed there were certainly changes. Plays were no longer divided into Acts because basically there wasn't any action. The New Drama split plays into propositions. The man with the most propositions thus became the most important playwright. In our case, this was G.B.S.H.A.W. – an Irish socialist of Scandinavian dramatology and German sociology, rescued by the Irish bit. That at least sprayed a bit of leprachaun levity about the place. But what about the sociology? Although intellectually appropriate to the West End, it does of course tend to grind one's play to an extremely boring halt.

Shaw overcame this lumpy ingredient in success after success. Through 'The Calculator', a play about V.A.T., to 'The Apple Tart', a tense drama of vegetarian living in North Finchley, right up to when God comes to review the universe for the Rent Tribunal, in 'Can We Afford It?', Shaw ably demonstrates that late capitalist society will masochistically pay lots of money to come and see itself blown to pieces by people with beards. However, our piece of Shavian Theatre is taken from 'Fingers and The Woman'.

(The curtain rises to reveal the drawing room of a consultancy in Harley Street, London W.1. It is 7 o'clock on a Wednesday evening in January 1908. A young woman, Julia Amazon, is seated upon the sofa-floral, Sanderson, recently washed, though not without a certain neurotic tension in the tautness of the covers. The lady is wearing a black Dutch Indonesian shawl which comes down to within one inch of her waist, and size 9 shoes. She has with her a dark brown holdall, resting at her feet, though the shoes should still be visible. Her gaze alternates between the holdall and Dr Mountebank in a sort of vaguely-timed pendulum. In all other respects she is able, confident, energetic, enigmatic, ridiculous and 28. Dr Mountebank is a consultant psychiatrist with a birthday in November and a wife in Honolulu. He is essentially authoritarian, bald and in his fifties. He has a son in the same room by the mantelpiece. This is Charles Mountebank. It is he who has evidently just caused a social hiatus by entering the room wearing a dinner jacket and a black eye-mask. Debonair, sharp and rather too tidy, he is 23 years and five months at the rising of the curtain. This should be made clear. The man who has come into the room with him is Fred Swipe, a colleague. He is, like Mountebank, in his fifties but a rather more corpulent burgher and dressed more strikingly in a hooped jersey. He too has a black eye-mask, and a packet of cigarettes behind his left ear. They are Anchor cigarettes. There are twelve of them.)

DR MOUNTEBANK: (*Looking forcefully at the holdall*) Well then Miss Amazon, my advice to you is to return this child to its rightful owner and come and see me again on Wednesday next, having discharged that duty.

JULIA: I do not see it as a duty. It isn't even strictly necessary – unless, that is, I feel like returning it so that I may take another one.

DR MOUNTEBANK: (*Enraged*) If that is your belief Miss Amazon, then psychiatry has no other solution for you, other than the police.

JULIA: And nor does society.

DR MOUNTEBANK: (*Puzzled*) Have you not heard of our eighth Commandment? 'Thou shalt not steal'.

JULIA: I do not consider it as stealing. I am in fact preventing further theft.

DR MOUNTEBANK: (*Collapsing into sofa*) Oh my God . . .

JULIA: (*Sensing her advantage*) It is to the police that you and I together should go for the sake of society's crimes against this poor woman.

DR MOUNTEBANK: (*Throws legs into air in despair*) Agh!

JULIA: (*Jumping on him*) Listen to me you bald pig. (*Makes herself comfortable on his larynx*) From the very first moment that poor wretched creature was brutally

165

forced to remake her husband in his own image, she was laying her life on the capitalist line. Cuts affecting the National Health Service show that she had a 1 in 40 chance of survival, and that while we are sitting here talking (*Mountebank starts choking*) that chance has diminished to 1 in 80. And to have weathered all that for a ball and chain! (*Mountebank struggles to indicate agreement*) She can't go back to work, and she can't afford not to. If her husband deserts her, then she has been deserted. Society has stolen that woman's life before anything I could do. But now there's something I can do. I left her a note in the pram. She will not do it all again.

(*Julia gets up slowly, though with considerably more speed than Mountebank finds for his ascent*)

DR MOUNTEBANK: You are a most forceful woman, Miss Amazon. I'm only glad that no chains and balls make themselves felt in the world quite as you do. (*He smoothes his waistcoat. The remains of a watch tumble out*) Have you got the time Charles?

CHARLES MOUNTEBANK: Yes. It is a quarter to seven. And we must be going soon. Father, allow me to present Frederick Swipe. He is a trained thief.

DR MOUNTEBANK: (*Laughing*) Some wag you are Charles! Good evening, Mr Swipe.

FRED SWIPE: 'Ullo. Nice little place you've got 'ere. That Sèvres is it, guv'nor?

DR MOUNTEBANK: How observant of you.

FRED SWIPE: Yeah. I can still pick 'em all right.

DR MOUNTEBANK: (*Gathering into mysterious incomprehension*) And where would you be going tonight?

CHARLES MOUNTEBANK: A working dinner party, Father. I take the coats, hand them to Fred, and then we leave. What harm does it do after all? There are plenty of people without wages and inside loos who could do with a coat. We only sell one or two to cover our expenses.

DR MOUNTEBANK: (*Stands up, looks at the other three, sighs deeply, adjusts his jacket and walks ponderously to the side wings. Shouts with great vehemence*) Oh God Shaw, give me some decent lines.

Meanwhile, in the dark throbbing fecund hand of D.H. Lawrence, the Novel nearly needed a white stick. However, before our discussion, please notice that Lawrence is not called David or Herbie or Larry Baby or anything like that. He might be sexy, but he's strictly D.H.

D. H. Lawrence was the result of a productivity deal between a miner and his wife. As such, he grew up to believe that the world was full of overpaid nancies, and that a day down the pit was necessary for a good shaft – or something like that. Accordingly, he began to stalk around the streets of Nottingham ogling young women from beneath a helmet, only to be convinced that Edwardian England was not catering for the provincial adolescent who wished to come across. Attitudes had to be changed. And what better place to begin than home? – where he proceeded to differ, and yet agree with his father, in the choice of his mother. This was the fault of industrial society. Improvements in transportation had now made it ridiculously tempting to whisk mum off. But Lawrence was nothing if not spontaneous, and left without her.

Presumably as something of a tribute to his background and beliefs, he married a German mother-of-three figure from Europe's most industrialised society and proceeded to take her everywhere – whilst perking up with a more legitimate sense of hatred for her father. Not that the marriage went smoothly, as is clear from the embittered 'Huns and Lovers' – transported from an earlier blistering vital draft, the eight-times-suppressed 'Sins and Livers'.

With this Lawrence set himself up as the high priest of love, and created some pretty well-proportioned characters. For example when Mellors the gamekeeper knocks Connie's teeth out and provides her with a pair of dentures, he is symbolically overcoming his fear of castration and not, as is sometimes argued, encouraging her to eat less. When Firkin Randy approaches Gudrun at the garden party scene of 'Women In Bed', he only has to say 'The rain is getting into my shoes, and my tie

feels tight' for her to understand at once and take her clothes off, and Firkin flee in terror remembering he'd left the dentures in his other suit.

There had to be a point at which society threw in the towel on Lawrence. And I think he knew this when publishers suddenly waxed a bit cool about 'Aaron's Rod'. Especially in the wake of complaints about 'Kangaroo'. But, alas, Lawrence was published and suppressed. Whether on grounds of obscenity or repetition we're not sure. All we do know is the Home Office solemnly dropped his novels over the White blistering hot throbbing fecund Cliffs of Dover into the vital, flowing sea.

Prose survived Lawrence and sailed on into the gay twenties where it met the Bloomsbury Group – very period, extremely gay and tremendous in their twenties. Bloomsbury is the name given to a more or less inextricable consortium of sisters, brothers, pooftahs, twins, sapphics and cousins who were all, by their own admission, brilliant. It all began when Virginia popped an ad into 'Chime Out': 'WANTED, TO PUMP UP DARING FLAT, related geniuses in loose flannel clothes willing to share

bathroom in exchange for light remarks'. The result was a troop of multisexual thinkers encamped at an ever-expanding address, such that a distinctive Bloomsbury voice was soon polishing the tiles, whipping up the fireplace and whistling round the chimney pots. In time of course everything went Bloomsbury: a Bloomsbury hat, a Bloomsbury walk, Bloomsbury underwear, Bloomsbury kitchen tiles, a Bloomsbury pet, even a superbly chiselled pirouettingly codaed Bloomsbury fart.

For the sake of convenience we shall be looking at their letters. I would also recommend in this context a close study of the 300 Volumes already on the market of 'The Unexpurgated Laundry Bills' by two people who'd vaguely heard of them, Lady Vaseline Bluebell and Ainsley Deck-Chair.

The Bloomsbury Round Robin

Dear Lytton,

Your brilliant letter! As I think you probably know I think you have absolutely the best mind in the western hemisphere since I stopped writing my novel two minutes ago. But of course you're right! Monk's House is a ménage à cinq. Only yesterday, poor dim wonderful Gresham called in to pour his heart out after the Japanese Lattice Work Exhibition, and incidentally try to go to bed with me. He really is in torments about Petunia, Dudley, Tessa and Clayton and would keep bursting into tears between being brilliant. I sometimes feel he is going to be the most amazing genius and write the most thrillingly perceptive book on Art – which he worships – but then at other moments I wonder if he isn't an absolute wanker. Seymour seduced Hartley by the way, and Violet is mysteriously pregnant. I think this is most unfortunate for her, feeling as she does about Bromley. Although they're married she has never really accepted him. If only someone would give him an aesthetic sense for I honestly see no other way in which he can acquire one. Come and have tea on Thursday. We can have a long walk together, and Duncan can do your portrait. The cat died yesterday. Woe Felix.

Yr.
V.W.

Dear Vaseline,

It's a great secret but I must tell you. Hartley and Seymour have become intimate. Apparently last weekend in Sussex a game of leapfrog got so out of hand that our two heroes experienced an Aristotelian moment in the asparagus bed. And all thanks to you! Oh how I envy you your genius in these matters, Vaseline! Oh to possess a quarter of your sublime vision! It was you who told Vanessa about leapfrog? She swears she found it in Rabelais; but I don't believe her. Anyway it's all for the good. Seymour's conversation desperately needs Hartley. Heard from Lytton by the way. Poor old Eight Legs! Still weaving his little web of history and having wet dreams about James I. What a wanker!

Yr.
V.W.

Dear Vaseline,

I shall be overjoyed to eat your food this weekend if I am well enough. However a cold seems to haunt me and quite crush my pen in the snivels. Must I be within your gates for the very first conversation? Could not some fair amanuensis keep a record for latecomers? Will little pink Hugh Wrigley be there I wonder? Virginia wrote to me by the way and said you were an idiot. Over four pages I exhausted myself in your defence. I sometimes wonder about old Nine Lives,

Yr.
Lytton.

Dear Lytton,

Only you know the pure joy in my heart at seeing you so well on the way to recovery last weekend. But really you mustn't believe what you vaguely think you half overhear from an eighth party. I most certainly don't think you're a wanker. On the contrary you have the most wonderful mind. Is Vaseline up to something with Petunia I wonder? I don't suppose you had time to see the way she handed her that croquet stick? Anyway wasn't little Hugh Wrigley nice? Is he really going to be Prime Minister? It would be such an awful waste. See you on Thursday for tea,

Yr.
V.W.

Prose had distinctly fewer blushing moments with its remaining artistes. Of whom there were approximately eleven. By a kind of co-incidence, they all came together for an innings of the Book Club, in its annual cricketing round with the Printers Union on August 4th, 1925. Shortly after the photographers had walked out, the Book Club won by default – the printers being unable to come up with an order which didn't seriously lower the batting standards of some of their members. Obliged, through mingled feelings of pride and self-protection, to bat all at once, or not at all, it was left, after an extended tea break, to the moonlighting Chairman of the Amalgamated Wicketkeepers and Longstops to deliver a note to the effect that the whole concept of a batting order was cricketingly divisive, and that the match had better be over by 4.30 anyway. The umpires, finding such over-productive over-manning of the wicket unacceptable, awarded victory with runs to the Book Club whose innings is recorded below with due deference to the expressed wish for anonymity of the printers.

GALSWORTHY c. Rent-Act, b. Coutts 62
WELLS stumped progress 33
KIPLING c.&b. Mowgli 50
HUXLEY emigrated [+?%]
JAMES (Capt.) c. Home Office, b. Inspector of Taxes Dec. Def.

BENNETT b. Literary Lion 6
FORSTER retired hurt 0
CHESTERTON not out 0
ORWELL c. Lenin, b. Stalin 13
WAUGH c. Marsh, b. Lillee 0
CONRAD ran aground 0

Poetry had a breather after Matthew Arnold and has come to be known as Georgian. This is a popular term of abuse roughly comparable with a weak gin and tonic. You can use it to describe anything from 1900–1918 which strikes you as missing the point. Once you know what the point is you can use it anywhere. However this label is generally considered unfair in the case of the War Poets who are widely acknowledged as having got the point. Looking down the list the big ones are Wilf Owen, Captain of the 1st Battalion of Welsh Poets, and Siegfried Sassoon, a Major in Counter-Intelligence Hairdressing.

The thing about the War Poets was that it didn't take them very long to get upset. Any thoughts about 'poor little Belgium' disappeared about as fast as you could say Common Market. Would they do the same for us was the question round the trenches, second only to 'Have you seen Chalky's leg?'. Poetic conditions were atrocious. It wasn't just the noise. It was all sorts of things: the bloke who wanted to tell you about his bird at home, the bloke who'd decided you'd be quite nice as his next bird, the 'England is great' lectures, the half-sozzled padre etc. It was, in a way, a sort of bloody miracle that anything got written at all. But Wilf saw it through.

By 1918 Poetry was knackered. In these circumstances it was most unwelcome to discover that poetic conditions in London had been made even more hazardous by the arrival of Ezra £.

Pound was an American, born in the Latin Quarter of Montana, the singularly random issue of Propertius and Clytemnestra Pound. He worked for a short time as Speculative Professor of Everything at the University of Idaho before finding himself on a one-way sabbatical to

London. Here he embarked upon a search of public libraries, art galleries and late-night movies looking for a woman called Dorothy Shakespeare. Excited by her literary echoes, he married her. They wasted no time in having a son, coyly suggesting a possible career for him in the choice of Virgil Goethe Confucius Rimbaud Wun Tun Pound. Pound believed in everything that was modern, continually exhorting 'Big Work, Right Now' in every manifesto that was going, from the Neo-Triangularist 'Blazing Tinkles' to the Neo-Volcanic 'Spurt'. When these all folded up he founded his own group, the Berlitz School of Poets, encouraging disciples only to read what he told them and write in personalised Esperanto. The climax of his own work was not just the magnificent 'Cantonese' but the creative amendments he made to other peoples' poems in his off-peak Chinese moments.

One poet who couldn't get his manuscript out of the way was T.S. Eliot. Eliot, originally an American, became a naturalised Englishman, whilst Pound remained a certified American. In the backlash of wanting to be English, Eliot actually started working for Lloyd's. But much to his disgust he still felt cut off. Staying late in his office with an umbrella, cup of coffee and a piece of cheese, he vented his apocalyptic sense of despair in a verbal film of the City entitled 'The Waste Gland' . . . with outside investments from £.

In the 1930's nobody was interested in Eliot, except those people who wanted to meet him. And only a few game souls were still trying to see what £ was on about. T.S. Eliot had gone into the Church and on holiday once to Spain, so as far as the Pylon Poets were concerned Eliot was 'off limits'. For what exactly was 'on limits' we shall have to meet our Pylon Poets.

Their leader was a sort of Marxist Biggles code-named 'Auden'. 'Auden' had come to London not knowing his way around until a friend gave him 'Das Kapital', which at least got him to the British Museum. Steeping himself in the lore of bygone ages, 'Auden' decided it was time

174

to destroy Western Civilisation. There were several brands of thought on the market capable of doing this but 'Auden' chose a German idea called Marxism. It had, quite rightly, singled out the workers as the people most likely to destroy civilisation, and 'Auden' began to feel that it was about time he met one. Contacts in the Electricity Board would arrange it. But where were 'the others'?

'The others' were in London too and had been sending in the more metrical passages of 'Das Kapital' to *Left Verse*, near Charing Cross Station. 'Auden' made his way there, in a light brown mac. When he flung open the trapdoor and looked down there were 'the others'. They were a friendly crowd and looked very intelligent in their sleeveless woollies. They showed him how to form a politically acceptable wrist and gave him a red shirt. He was to see 'them' again on many occasions. Usually one at a time, over Gitanes and cocoa by the fireside where to fantasise with a politically reliable friend in a sleeveless woolly about 'the struggle' was all the rage. By 1934 there were less reds under the bed than in it.

Still, it transpired as he worked his way through 'them' that 'they' hadn't seen a worker either. Contacting the Electricity Board again 'Auden' requested that more equipment be laid on as he was bringing some friends. Their mission details arrived three days later. They were to leave London and head twenty-five miles southwest into the countryside where they would be allowed to take over the construction of a pylon. The day has gone down in electrical history.

It wasn't such a good game after all this Marxism. You could do yourself an injury. And the language when 'Auden' had put the tractor through its paces was nothing if not proletarian, though not exactly fraternal. Loud remarks about the bourgeoisie's ability to destroy civilisation, if not couched in precisely that way, had put 'Auden' and his friends quite off 'the struggle' for a night or two.

Yet still they wrote. Poems about pylons gave way, most ambitiously, to ones about air hangars, customs' sheds even, heaven forbid, weapons' factories. But no-one took any notice anyway. And Orwell was continually stressing that we needed communism like a hole in the head, which has subsequently proved to be one of the best ways of looking forward to it. If only Karl had made some of his own money instead of arranging for its removal from others, 'x' million might be a lot better off, 'y' million still alive and 'z' million at least free to read this book.

German ideas went rather out of fashion in 1939. 'Auden' left with his friend for America – 'they' taking Poetry and something of the novel with them. 'The others' mostly did a quick left-right, generally becoming sky pilots of some description in the process. What remained of Poetry and the novel stayed on to fight it out, whilst Drama, with the lights out and bombs exploding all around it, knew that it was time for another rest.

And so our story arrives at 1939, at which point over 2000 years of Eng. Lit. have gone before you reader. I would like to join with Dr Duff Wimpole in hoping that you can now pick 4 questions in 2½ hours. If not, I'd go back to the beginning. But you'll be on your own. We have to lecture on Blake at 10.30.

Appendix

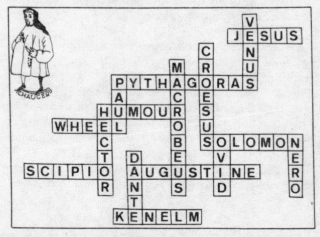